THE GUIDE TO PASSIVE INCOME

THE GUIDE TO
PASSIVE
INCOME

How Affluent Investors
Build Generational Wealth

ANDREW LANOIE

with Andy Earle

For everyone who has mentored me.

Table of Contents

Foreword

By Ken McElroy

There are certain people in every walk of life for whom success comes effortlessly. They somehow seem to be involved in great deals, connected to the best people, and aware of interesting opportunities. Without working themselves to death, they enjoy the fruits of their labor, prestige, and respect. Their friends and family adore them, and they glide through life with smiles on their faces. They give back to their friends and communities and are well-known and admired among their neighbors. It's tempting to chalk these outrageous success stories up to family connections or simply being in the right place at the right time. But that's not the whole story.

Andrew Lanoie is a perfect example. His focus on alternative investments and residential real estate not only creates opportunities and passive income for his investors, but for hard working Americans desperately in need of safe, clean, and affordable housing.

You might be aware of Andrew from his top-rated, *The Impatient Investor*, where he breaks down the secret wealth strategies of the 0.1%. But I've known him personally for over ten years. We met before I wrote my book, *The Sleeping Giant*, through a real estate education group that I was part of, and I wanted to learn what he was doing. We bonded over a mutual love of music and real estate.

Over the years I've heard stories, like how he was almost the bass player for the band Linkin Park, but became a Talent Agent at William Morris instead. I also heard the one about how his rock band sold 100,000 records before he'd even graduated from high school. And he's got tons of great tales from the 16 years he spent representing celebrities like Tom Petty, Steve Martin, Tony Bennett and Taylor Swift. It's never a bad idea to make friends with a William Morris agent.

Andrew's book, *Passive Income*, finally gave me the opportunity to peek behind the curtain. In these pages he systematically walks through every major type of passive income producing asset, explains how they work, and shows you how to use them in your portfolio. It goes well beyond the stock market or the real estate market and addresses the entire landscape of passive income investing.

If you want to build recurring streams of revenue so you can replace your salary, quit your job, and live a stress-free life of abundance and inner peace, this book is for you.

If you want to safeguard yourself for retirement, so you can relax and feel confident that your portfolio can sustain you and your family after you leave your job, this book is for you.

If you have been mindlessly contributing to a 401k or company sponsored retirement plan without much thought, and you're ready to take control of your financial life, this book is for you.

If you're simply curious to learn more about how passive income works so you can make more informed decisions about your savings plan in the future, this book is for you.

You've made an excellent choice by picking up a copy of Andrew Lanoie's *Passive Income*. There are many books out there from many so-called experts, and you have managed to locate one of the true gems. I hope you enjoy.

Sincerely,

Ken McElroy

How I Live On Passive Income

In my twenties I had one of the best jobs on the planet in terms of salary, perks, and lifestyle, but I felt like I was trapped on a never-ending hamster wheel with no control over my own life. The turning point came when I realized that the key to achieving true independence was passive income. I became obsessed with a crazy idea: What if I could build up enough automatic monthly revenue to completely replace my lavish salary, so I could quit my job and take control of my life without taking a dip in cashflow?

Five years later I'd done it—so I resigned. And I never looked back. Now, in this book I'm sharing the exact strategy that I used.

When I first got the idea to focus on passive income I was working at William Morris, the largest talent agency in the world. I represented celebrities like Tim Allen, Taylor Swift, Steven Spielberg, Steve Martin, and many others. My salary placed me in the top 1% of wage earners nationwide; the company washed, waxed, fueled, and paid for my BMW every week; and I hung out with Peter Frampton, Barry Manilow, and David Hasselhoff on the weekends (at least, when I wasn't partying at the Playboy Mansion). I felt like I was living in my wildest dreams.

But then I received a serious wake-up call.

Literally, my friend's dad called me at 7am—and it woke me up. I had known my buddy's dad, Bob, since I was a kid. To me, he had been one of those guys who seemed to have it all figured out: he married a wonderful woman, had a string of four kids, and made a good enough living that he was able to retire early to a luxury condo on the beach in Boca Raton. He even planned an extended three-month Mediterranean cruise with his wife and somehow managed it all with his two youngest daughters still in college.

Bob was two months into his retirement and seven months out from his grand European adventure when he called me in a complete panic. It was 2008 and the global financial meltdown was in full swing. He told me his stock portfolio had dropped 30% overnight. He whispered that he had no clue how he was going to tell his wife that the money he'd worked so hard to save was evaporating before his eyes. Expenses were piling up. How could he afford the forthcoming property tax payments on the condo? How would he pay for the next three years of tuition for his girls? Christ, could he even afford Europe anymore? This had been their dream vacation for the past 25 years. He was talking about going back to work.

Bob had heard that I just started to dabble in real estate investments and he thought, just maybe, I could help him find the right investments to turn it all around. I started to do some research and learned my friend's dad wasn't alone (far from it, actually). National statistics show Americans close to retirement have an average nest egg of just 2.4 times their current income, nowhere near the 8 times prescribed by financial experts. And a full 45% of Baby Boomers have no retirement savings whatsoever.

I took a look at my own finances and realized I was falling into the same traps as Bob. I had a company-sponsored 401k, but beyond a few real estate investments here and there, I hadn't given much thought to what it would actually take to achieve true financial independence. Naively, I'd' assumed the company would take care of my finances in the same way they took care of everything else.

But I was wrong.

After that call from Bob, I became obsessed with passive income. I contacted mentors, went to seminars, and joined networking groups. Within six months, I was able to help my friend's dad turn his financial situation around. The Mediterranean getaway was a go. The condo was set. His girls wouldn't have to worry about applying for financial aid. Next, I shifted my efforts to my own finances and within 5 years I was making more from my investments than my agency salary. That's when I quit my job to start investing full time.

Today, I head up my own investment firm. I have clarity about what I'm investing in and the security of knowing I'll be protected, even if the markets change. And I've got more free time than I ever had before.

The moment everything started to click for me came when I was working to solve my friend's dad's (Bob's) financial problems back in late 2008. Pouring over a spreadsheet of monthly costs and expenditures, I realized he had completely focused on the wrong thing. He put all his energy into overall portfolio value, not into generating cash flow. Bob needed passive income.

The way many of us grew up thinking about wealth is outdated. We still use phrases like "millionaire," "money in the bank," and "trust funder" to describe rich people, but the days when you could park a chunk of money in a savings account and earn 10% interest are over. Today, money doesn't do you much good sitting around collecting dust. Being a "millionaire" doesn't mean you're set for life. Actually, in a current savings account, a million dollars would pay out less than $5,000 per year—hardly something to live on.

How much guaranteed income would you need every month in order to feel secure? Don't set your sights too low. Forty-four percent of Boomers report thinking they'll be able to live on less than $35,000 a year after they retire. In reality, however, the average American aged 65 to 74 burns through upwards of $55,000 and that number is rising fast. Social Security, on the other hand, pays out just a little over $1,000 per month on average. Where's the rest of the money going to come from? And what if you want to live an above-average life after retirement? What if you plan to spend more than $55,000? Or to retire early, maybe at age 45?

Passive income is the answer. It worked for Bob. It worked for me. And now it's working for my clients. When I say "passive income" I'm talking about investments that pay you every month or quarter without requiring any time or effort. That doesn't mean picking up some Uber routes, flipping things on eBay, starting a YouTube channel, Etsy Store, makeup blog, or taking surveys online. These activities all require time and effort. By definition, they aren't passive.

What I'm talking about is truly *passive* income. The kind you can quite literally make in your sleep. The kind that trickles into your account each month or each quarter regardless of whether or not you get out of bed. It's only by generating this kind of income that you can achieve the type of financial freedom and wealth to enjoy life on your own terms. With passive income, you can stop living a life of worry and start living one filled with abundance, confidence, and tranquility.

To create real significant wealth there are about a dozen passive income strategies I see working for savvy investors in today's market. Even within these options, there are a few I can recommend more highly than the rest because I've experienced success with them, seen them work well for others, and the numbers work out particularly well right now.

Passive Income Generating Assets:

1. Fixed Income (Bonds and Treasuries)
2. Savings / CD's / Money Market
3. Dividend Stocks
4. Private Equity

5. Active Real Estate Investing

6. Secured Private Real Estate Lending

7. Indirect Real Estate Investing (REITs)

8. Crowdfunding Real Estate

9. Peer-to-Peer Lending

10. Annuities

11. Angel Investing

Notice I didn't include Bitcoin or the hottest new tech IPO on this list. Yes, people make money from doing those things. You could triple your investment if you happen to pick a winner, but you still won't make a cent until you decide to sell your shares or "cash out."

Any type of investment that requires you to work in order to get paid is not truly passive. In the stock market, there is definitely money to be made. However, you have to constantly buy and sell stocks in order to earn income. The exception to this is dividend stocks, which I'll cover in-depth in this book.

These pages contain the exact strategies I use with my team at Four Peaks Partners to consistently make outsized returns for our clients. I decided to give away everything I've learned about passive income because I want to help new investors who can't afford the six-figure minimum to get involved in one of my funds. If you scrupulously apply the ideas I share in this book, you'll be there soon. And when you are, let's talk. I'll be waiting for you.

CHAPTER 1

Background, Mindset, and Myths

Jerry Seinfeld wasn't out of his mind when he turned down CBS's unprecedented offer of $5 million per episode to shoot a tenth season of his eponymous show. Jerry didn't need to work for a fixed salary anymore because he'd shifted his focus from active income to passive income. Just a few years previously, *Seinfeld* had entered syndication, which put Jerry in a unique position. The comedian was not only the show's main star, he was also the creator, executive producer, and head writer. This combination means that Jerry earns a much greater share of the show's royalties than any other TV star.

Jerry saw there was much more money to be made by signing syndication and licensing deals for his show than there would be in filming more episodes. Over the next ten years Jerry sat back and collected royalties. By 2015, the show had grossed over $3.1 billion—the majority of which found its way right into the comedian's already bulging pockets. That same year Seinfeld signed a six-year deal with Hulu for the rights to stream his show online until 2021. The Hulu contract brings in an estimated $400 million per year—most of which, again, goes directly to Jerry.

Beginning in 2021, as soon as the Hulu deal runs out, Seinfeld will be made available on Netflix. The details of this new contract have not been publicized, but sources indicate Netflix outbid Hulu, Amazon, WarnerMedia, NBCUniversal, and Viacom for the right to stream the show. Insiders have reported the dollar amount for this deal is considerably larger than even the Hulu contract.

In other words, Jerry Seinfeld is set for life.

Of course, we can't all create, produce, write, and star in one of the most beloved shows of all time. Most of us aren't hilarious, well-connected, or Jewish enough to be the next Seinfeld. But that doesn't mean we can't all earn enough passive income to be set for life in exactly the same way as Jerry.

It is not merely possible. In my world, it's fairly common.

And no, I'm not an "online marketer" or an "internet entrepreneur." I'm not going to tell you to start a YouTube channel or write an ebook. Those kinds of tactics might make sense for Millennials, fitness models, or bored housewives with hours of free time and no starting capital. But the types of sophisticated investors I work with at my firm, Four Peaks Partners, are looking for more of a set-it-and-forget-it approach.

I decided to write this book because I took a look at all of the books, videos, and courses out there on the topic of passive income and realized they are all full of cheesy tactics bordering on scams. Unless you're interested in drop-shipping Amazon purchases for twenty-five cents a package, don't waste your time.

Most of the books and articles I found on passive income start off with the inspiring story of Pat Flynn, the architect who was laid off in 2008 and decided to create a website to help him study for the Leadership in Energy and Environmental Design (LEED) exam. Just a few months after launching his website, it started to generate thousands of unique visits every day. He received emails from grateful visitors all over the world saying things like, "Pat, your stuff is nice, I would pay for it!" At that point, Pat realized that he didn't have to wait around for a call from LEED. He could take his financial future into his own hands.

Soon, Pat had authored an ebook study guide, which he started selling for $19.99. At the end of his first month, he had made $7,008. Next, he created a YouTube Channel and podcast. Then he launched three other websites. Amazingly, Pat has made $3 million in the last six years strictly from "passive income."

What an incredible success!

Except...Pat's income doesn't sound all that passive to me. In fact, building numerous websites from scratch, writing ebooks, hosting a podcast, shooting YouTube videos, and managing a collection of social media channels actually sounds like a full-time job. Would Pat continue to earn the same $500k per year if he stopped working around the clock on his businesses? Maybe. But probably not.

Also, Pat's magical success story skates over another important fact: 98% of all websites never earn any money or achieve any significant level of traffic. I strongly believe in checking out the numbers closely before diving into any potential investment. And starting a YouTube channel is not a sound investing strategy—sorry.

If you go back and read Pat's inspiring story again, you'll notice that even Pat Flynn himself didn't start his site as an investment. He started it as a hobby. It was something he did for fun, to keep himself occupied while he studied for the LEEDS exam. Only after he noticed that the site was receiving thousands of visitors per day did he begin attempting to monetize it.

In other words: he got lucky.

I sincerely hope that you get lucky too and a lucrative stream of web traffic falls right into your lap. If it does, then by all means write an ebook. But until then, focus on the strategies that are based on numbers and don't require luck.

You don't have to get lucky at all to earn passive income. Passive income investing is quite simple. It's about holding onto certain types of assets for many years and collecting checks while your investments generate periodic distributions, known as **dividends** or **disbursements**. Then, you can take these checks and use them to purchase even more assets. Round and round it goes until you own a massive portfolio that generates millions of dollars per year without requiring any time, energy, or attention at all.

At least, that's how I define passive income!

In my work, I've seen motivated people go from $0 in passive income to tens of thousands per week. It isn't necessarily easy to generate passive income, but it also isn't particularly complicated. Passive income investing is based on simple math that a fifth grader can understand. In these chapters, I'm going to break down exactly how it works and how I approach it.

No matter what your current circumstances are, you can become wildly successful by shifting your focus to prioritize the right types of passive income-generating assets. I can show you how to make your money work for you instead of the other way around. The right investing strategy can save you from years of slow progress and unnecessary failures.

But before any of that, the first step is a mindset shift. It might seem simple, but it's profound and important. You need to commit to the idea of building passive income. You need to decide that maximizing your automated cashflow is a top priority in your life. This isn't going to be "effortless". It's not going to just "happen" without some serious work. Make a promise to yourself that you'll put in the time.

Once you set up an automatic money machine to generate recurring revenue for you each month for the rest of your life, you'll be freed up to focus your time and energy on other goals you might want to pursue. Instead of spending forty hours per week at your job, you can spend that time on...well, anything you want.

If you're reading this, I know you're at least interested in the possibility of generating passive income. I hope to convince you to make it one of your top goals. But first, I have to quickly show you that the entire way you've been thinking about your financial portfolio up until now is completely wrong. And I'll reveal how you should be thinking about it instead.

Financial Myths of Novice Investors

"Buy low, sell high" is one of the most popular, basic, and universally-accepted pieces of financial wisdom on the planet, and I've noticed that most novice investors simply accept it without question. But it turns out this basic truism of sound investing is a complete myth. The phrase implies we should earn money on every investment by selling it for more than we paid. On its surface, "buy low, sell high" seems obvious. *Yeah, of course you have to make money on your investments to be a successful investor. Duh.*

However, in truth, "buy low, sell high" is an outdated mentality and there are big problems with trying to blindly apply this logic to every situation in today's economy. Many of the richest people on the planet have never bought anything low or sold anything high in their lives, but yet they are extravagantly wealthy (many of these people are my clients, actually).

Let's walk through a basic example of this principle so you can see what I'm talking about here.

Passive Income Example:

1. Chad buys a two-bedroom apartment for $200,000 with $50,000 down
2. He immediately finds a tenant and begins renting it out for $2,000 a month

5

3. Chad earns $600 per month profit after paying his mortgage and property taxes
4. Five years later, the market crashes and the value drops to $150,000 (a loss of 25%)
5. Chad has gained some equity during the five years, so he refinances his loan
6. He is able to withdraw $40,000 cash and he uses it to buy a second apartment
7. With property taxes dropping, Chad's monthly passive income jumps to $1,400

So is Chad a savvy investor or a moron? Well, he certainly didn't "buy low," because the value of his investment actually went down after he bought it. And he also definitely did not "sell high." Actually, he never sold the apartment at all. Today, Chad owns hundreds of apartments all over the country and he earns tens of thousands of dollars each week without lifting a finger. He has never sold a single apartment in his entire investing career.

"Buy low, sell high" is one of those sayings that's easy to accept without question. Because we've heard it so many times, it starts to just feel true. But it's actually an ancient and flawed way of thinking. When you adopt the buy-low-sell-high mindset, your main focus becomes chasing one-time profits. This means you'll be attracted to investments with a high upside, i.e. potential to increase in value, such as promising biotech companies, popular IPOs, and visionary startups. For instance, you might have invested in companies like Facebook, Twitter, Amazon, and Google back in their early days.

However, those types of investments are extremely risky. And they don't pay dividends. For every Facebook and Twitter there are a thousand failed companies like Bolt, Everloop, Focus.com, Friendster, Kiwibox, MemeStreams, Musical.ly, Raptr, Spring.me, So.cl, Tribe.net, YikYak, and many others. Luck and timing have to be on your side to pick the next Facebook, and even if you do, when do you sell it? Do you sell when it's up 100%? Or wait until it's up 200%?

Let's say you are in the absolute best possible situation that any buy-low-sell-high devotee could possibly find themselves: you invested $10,000 in Facebook just a few months after their initial offering back in 2012, when the price was down to $17.73 per share. Four years later, in 2016, the price is up to $132 per share, meaning your $10,000 is now worth $74,450! So, should you sell it? Maybe. But, then again, it's going to be worth $138,200 four years later in 2020. And who knows what it will be worth in another four years by 2024…

When you use the buy-low-sell-high approach, your work is never done. You might sell your Facebook stock in 2020 for a gain of nearly 14x, but then what? Do you spend the money? Purchase a new investment? Spend half and reinvest the rest? The decisions (and opportunities to make a wrong move) are never-ending. And that's in the absolute best-case scenario where you invested in Facebook at the perfect time! More often than not the price goes down and you lose money on an investment.

On the other hand, Chad never had to deal with any of these difficult choices. He simply bought an apartment, found a tenant, and collected his rent every month. In fact, even though the apartment actually lost value, he still made money every month. Chad's story proves that there are serious flaws to the idea of buying low and selling high. It might work in some cases, but it certainly isn't the only approach (and I would argue it isn't even a good one).

A second myth most novice investors won't question: "a penny saved is a penny earned." It's a classic financial utterance originally attributed to Benjamin Franklin that feels not only wise, but also strangely patriotic. However, when we look deeper, this phrase, too, has serious problems behind it. The big assumption Franklin makes is that the success of your portfolio is directly tied to its overall value. Back in his day, with guaranteed interest rates of over 10% per year, that may have been true. But today simply saving your money isn't good enough. You also have to put your savings to work generating revenue (like Chad did).

Another money-related truism is, "a fool and his money are soon parted." This adage, too, involves numerous assumptions. For example, that others will take advantage of you if you give them the chance. However, most financial advisors, brokers, and accountants are honest and hard-working people (plus, they are regulated up the wazoo and couldn't screw you over if they wanted). Another assumption inherent in this phrase is that wisdom and careful thought are the best ways to avoid being taken advantage of. But some of the world's best investors rely on instinct to sniff out the next deal. And studies show going with your "gut" can often be more accurate than careful, deliberate thinking. So, this myth doesn't check out either.

Throughout your life, well-meaning people have been parroting these harmful ideas about money back to you. You've heard phrases like "buy low, sell high," "a penny saved is a penny earned," and "a fool and his money are soon parted"—along with others like "money doesn't grow on trees" and "don't count your chickens before they've hatched"—thousands of times. It's impossible not to internalize some inaccurate and conflicting messages about money.

Maybe you've bought into the assumption that you'll need to scrimp and save in order to become wealthy. Or you might have internalized the idea that wealthy people take advantage of others, or that the only way to get rich is by investing in stocks, or that you'll have to work 100 hours per week to get ahead. These assumptions come from many places, including the expressions we hear and messages we see in the media related to money and success. The conditioning happens so gradually, over the course of many years, that we don't even notice it.

In my opinion, the most harmful attitude many people have about money is defining success by the dollar amount in your portfolio. If you ask the average person about her portfolio, you'll probably get a response like, "It's worth $625,000," or, "I'm up 20% this year!" And that is certainly one way to measure success. But if you asked my clients that same question, you'd get an answer like, "It's producing $73,000 per month." We don't focus on overall size because size is not what truly matters when it comes to your lifestyle. Instead, we focus on monthly passive income. That's our success metric.

Even if you're making plenty of money buying low and selling high right now, there will come a time when you'll want to be able to sit back, stop working so hard, and live comfortably off your investment income. In order to do this you're going to have to broaden your strategy. You're going to have to drop the "buy low, sell high" mentality and start measuring success in terms of your monthly passive cashflow. This is the way to true financial freedom.

Take an honest look at your current investment portfolio through this new lens. How successful have you been? How much passive cashflow are your investments generating each month right now? Don't be hard on yourself. It's important to know where you stand. Raising this number will be your new goal.

In this book, I'm going to explore the top eleven types of passive income generating assets. In the coming chapters I'll break down how each type works and how to decide which strategies will work best for you. I'll reveal how I built my own massive portfolio that generates millions in annual passive income. You'll also see how I was almost a member of the band Linkin Park, and I'll tell you about a huge mistake I made early on in my investing career—and what I did to fix it. Most importantly, I'll explain how I developed my unique philosophy of investing and what sets my approach apart from other passive income systems.

The Day that Changed My Financial Life

I didn't know I was going to be a passive income investor when I grew up. As a kid I wanted to be a rock star, and by the time I was in high school I was well on my way. The band I formed with three of my classmates, called "GrooveChild," had gained a small following in New Hampshire and surrounding states. We'd been performing in regional battle-of-the-bands competitions for a couple years and our demo album, "Children of the Groove," was doing well.

But we wanted more.

While my band mates focused their attention on writing us a full-length album, I got to work on managing the business side of things. I studied other successful local and regional acts, looked at what the biggest bands in our area had done to become popular, and put together a plan for how we could market our music in exactly the same way. The key, I realized, was to break into playing the college circuit and get as much radio airplay as possible.

Every day after school while other kids tinkered with their cars, went to sports practice, and smoked reefer, I hit the phones. I called every bar, club, music venue, college, and high school within 500 miles. Most of the time, they hung up on me or told me to get lost. But every now and then my calls resulted in a booking. I kept detailed records of everyone who booked us so I could follow up with them later about potentially booking us again. I also called every radio station and college radio station on the East Coast to pitch them on adding our music to their lineup. At a few smaller stations I was able to get through to some DJs, who asked me to send over a sample of our music, which at the time, meant mailing a cassette tape.

Our full-length album, *Sick at Last*, was finished in 1992 and I immediately sent copies to all of the club, bar, and radio contacts I'd been gathering. Then I called all of them a few days later to follow up. This resulted in a wave of new bookings and, even more importantly, some radio airtime. A few college stations had started playing one of our songs, a tune called "Riverside," off the new album—and it was catching on at our live shows too.

Soon we were playing three or four shows a week all around the greater New Hampshire region. We'd hit Portland, Maine, and Boston once a month, Providence and New York every 45 days, and a handful of college campuses in Pennsylvania and New Jersey in between. The college radio stations I'd been in contact with were giving our songs a lot of airtime. Then a larger regional station, WHEB, in Portsmouth, New Hampshire, started playing "Riverside" too—and listeners loved it. At one point, "Riverside" was the station's number-one most requested song for seven consecutive weeks.

We were booking consistent shows and getting airplay, had sold over 100,000 copies of **Sick at Last**, and were beating out larger national artists on the Billboard charts. Critics started referring to our style as a new genre, "Biker Jazz." A record deal seemed like the next logical step and the record companies who contacted us agreed.

But it wasn't to be.

We felt all of the offers we received posed a serious threat to our creative freedom. Beyond that, from a business perspective, they didn't make sense. There was a lot of stress wondering if we would make the wrong decision or throw away something big. We decided not to sign a record deal and continued to tour for a while as an independent band, but by the time I was 22 I realized my true passion was in the business of selling records, not making them.

I moved to Hollywood and used those same skills I'd developed cold-calling nightclub owners and radio DJs all up and down the East Coast to get a job in the music industry. I called every record label and talent agency in Los Angeles, told them my story, and asked what I could do to become a music executive. Impressed by my hustle and real-word experience selling over 100,000 records, some of the people I got in touch with were willing to give me a chance. I wound up with a job at William Morris, the top talent agency in the world.

For a few years I devoted my entire life to the agency, working around the clock and never taking a day off. In return, I was promoted quickly. I soon had the type of career most people dream of; one most parents ride their kids hard to achieve. I represented some of the top entertainers and musicians in the world. I had a company car. I hung out with celebrities. I was living "the dream." I worked harder, was promoted more, and started to get comfortable.

That's when the 2008 financial crash hit and I woke up to the panicked early-morning call from my friend's dad, Bob, who was losing his savings. I looked hard at my own finances and realized I'd made the same mistakes he had. The loss put me face-to-face with a cold reality. My company-sponsored retirement account was at the mercy of Wall Street and, worse yet, I didn't truly understand any of the assets I was investing in. I was blindly putting money into my 401k and the stock market. For years, I'd been going along with what I thought everyone was "supposed" to do, trusting it would work out. But I had no idea where my money was actually going, and no concrete plan to achieve financial independence.

So I started searching.

In 2009 I met a real estate mogul who introduced me to the world of real estate investing. He pulled back the curtain on his deals, showed me how they worked, and introduced me to the concept of *passive income*. I spent a full year studying every piece of academics and advice he threw at me. I met as many people in the real estate world as I could, asked lots of questions, and tried to learn the ropes. I saw that successful real estate investors all had long-term passive cash flow, and that excited me.

But how could I get started?

My mentor told me about something called the "1% Rule," which states that if you can rent a house out for 1% of its value each month, it should be able to generate cash flow immediately. So, I did the same thing I'd done in high school: I started calling people all over the country. I contacted real estate agents, property managers, and developers to compare property values and rent prices in different areas for various types of real estate. I looked at commercial properties, office buildings, apartments, and single-family homes.

After much research, I settled on single-family homes in Dallas, Texas. In 2009, you could get a house outside of Dallas for $125,000, with 20% down, and it would rent for about $1,500 per month. The math was obvious: $1,500 is more than 1% of $125,000. That meant the investment was immediately cash flow positive. I bought my first house, and after paying the mortgage every month it generated $400 of passive income. When I got that first check it suddenly clicked for me. I realized that I could do exactly the same thing again and make $800 per month. Then I could do it again and make $1,200.

Next, I put together a 5-year plan to purchase enough real estate to completely replace my agency salary with passive income. I ended up doing it in about four years. During that time, I bought over a hundred single-family homes. It was a surreal moment when my passive income actually surpassed my agency salary. It was hard to believe that I could suddenly make more money doing nothing than I made at one of the highest-paid jobs in the world.

In 2013, I left William Morris. It was a triumphant moment. Although most of my friends and colleagues couldn't wrap their heads around exactly what I was doing, many were interested. They saw that I'd climbed out of the corporate sinkhole and was now the captain of my own life, setting my sails with absolute freedom. Though many still thought I was crazy for leaving my "dream job," most expressed jealousy. They wanted to know how I'd done it. Given so much interest, I opened an investment group and we grew quickly.

Today, Four Peaks Partners manages a massive portfolio of homes and developments for a growing list of wealthy investors. I get to be highly selective about who I work with, I do what I love, and I have more than enough passive income to set myself and my family up for the rest of our lives.

The most common question people ask me is how they can build more passive income for themselves. Of course, investing with Four Peaks is the best way (shameless plug), but if you can't afford our minimum contribution yet, or, if you want to explore other types of income-producing assets, you can learn everything you need to know in the coming pages.

In the next chapter I'll get started with the first type of asset: Fixed Income. But first, let's talk about the second richest man of all time...

Video Assignment #1: Where Vanderbilt Went Wrong

At the end of each chapter, I'll recommend a related video aimed at deepening your understanding of passive income and provide valuable insights for growing your generational wealth. I recommend you take the time to watch each video before proceeding to the next chapter.

In this chapter, I shared my journey and how I learned to lay the foundation for financial freedom for myself and my family. What can happen if you don't invest in creating those passive revenue streams? Believe me, it can be a lot worse than what happened to Bob.

In this video I share a cautionary tale about the importance of a steady passive income stream. Cornelius Vanderbilt was the second richest man ever to live, but his family squandered his vast fortune in the span of a century after his death. In spite of his tremendous wealth Vanderbilt failed to secure his assets, ultimately paving the way for his family to ruin his financial and intellectual legacy.

To access the video, go to passiveincomethebook.com/1.

CHAPTER 2

Fixed Income

When most people think of fixed income securities (such as bonds), they tend to imagine something antiquated, like an investment their grandparents might have made during the Great Depression. But the highest-paid individual in all of human history would disagree.

In 1970, a 24-year-old recent business school graduate, Michael Milken, was hired by New York investment bank Drexel Firestone as their new "Director of Low-Grade Bond Research." He was given a small allowance of $2 million to trade with. During his first year, Milken doubled it to $4 million. His stunned managers immediately gave him more capital and during the next year he doubled it again. Over the following five years Milken was promoted multiple times and was soon running his own high-yield bond trading department within the company, continuing to make 100% returns every year. By 1976 he was receiving personal payments of over $5 million.

Milken's bond-trading department at Drexel Firestone (as well as his personal income) continued to climb astronomically in the next decade. Because of his unique compensation agreement with Drexel, in which he earned 50% of all profits he generated for the company, Milken's salary grew higher and higher each year as capital poured into the low-grade bonds market. In 1986 he was paid nearly $295 million. Then, the following year, Milken took home $550 million. According to a recent analysis, this is the highest compensation any individual has ever earned during a single year. It's more than Bill Gates, John D Rockefeller, or Andrew Carnegie ever made—even after adjusting for inflation.

How did Milken earn more money in one year than anyone else in recorded history? He found a way to get rich trading high-yield bonds. It might not sound glamorous or sexy, but Milken mastered fixed income and made it work for himself and his clients in a way that led to the creation of an incredible amount of new wealth.

Milken's fascination with high-yield bonds didn't come out of the blue. It had started years earlier during his undergraduate business studies at UC Berkeley. It was there where Milken was first introduced to W. Braddock Hickman's work of the 1940s and 1950s. Hickman was an economist and former president of the Federal Reserve Bank of Cleveland. His work suggested to Milken that a portfolio of non-investment grade bonds could be highly profitable, even compared to a standard investment-grade portfolio. Milken was taken with Hickman's ideas and was dying to test them out.

At the Wharton School of Business, Milken wrote his thesis on the bond rating system and the huge opportunity presented by some of the most poorly-rated bonds, known as "low-grade bonds." These were issued by companies that had originally received a favorable "AAA" rating but were currently rated an unfavorable "BBB" (or worse). What Milken realized was that the market was significantly overestimating the likelihood these companies would fail to meet their obligations. Because these bonds were considered "risky," no one wanted to get near them. But Milken saw an opportunity.

As he predicted, these "risky" bonds turned out to be highly profitable for Drexel Firestone. When large numbers of bonds were bundled together the risk of default was mitigated. The high interest rates these debtors were obligated to pay—because of their poor credit—meant the many who did pay made up for the few who couldn't. Companies in need of capital flocked to Milken for help issuing bonds. Investors with mountains of cash lined up to purchase their own bundles of high-yield bonds for passive income. Milken made millions by issuing the bonds himself and selling them to the hordes of hungry investors. He used fixed income securities to eventually turn that original $2 million into a vast fortune.

The majority of Americans can't define what fixed income investing is or how it works. In a recent survey of over 2,000 Americans, only 8% were correctly able to define "fixed income investing." Even though this vehicle is responsible for creating the highest annual income in all of human history, most people don't know the first thing about it, and fewer still have a deep understanding of how to put this powerful passive income tool to work in their own lives.

On a basic level, all fixed income investments are centered around debt. They generally include a coupon payment every month, or every six months, for the duration of the security along with the return of the principal on or before the maturation date.

For example, when you take out a mortgage in order to buy your dream home, the bank will generously give you every penny of the money upfront. All you have to do in exchange is agree to make some small payments each month, for the next thirty years, until the entire amount is paid back, plus interest, without ever missing a payment. You might look at the transaction as a way of making an investment in your home, but from the bank's perspective, they just made an investment in you. You've become a passive income stream for the bank. And because you've agreed to pay the bank a fixed amount each month for a fixed period of time, this entire arrangement would fall under the category of "fixed income."

The key to making this investment class work for you is to be on the other side of the equation. You don't want to be the one making the payments each month (like when you take out a mortgage). You want to be the one receiving the payments (like the bank). In other words, a mortgage is backwards. In order for fixed income to be an investment, it needs to be flipped. You'll be in the role of the bank, lending out money upfront in exchange for guaranteed income on a fixed schedule in return.

The safest type of fixed income instrument is the treasury bill, or T-Bill. This is debt issued by the U.S. federal government and it is highly trustworthy, liquid, and secure. Because these investments are so secure, their return is not high. When you buy a T-Bill, you are essentially loaning money to the government and they are promising to pay you interest payments every six months ("coupon" payments) and then return your principal when the bond reaches maturity.

Corporate bonds are issued by private companies seeking to raise capital for various acquisitions, expansions, and projects. Each company that issues a bond is rated and the bond receives a score. Highly scored bonds are considered safe and are given lower interest rates. On the other hand, bonds with less favorable scores may be classified as "junk bonds," resulting in higher interest.

What Milken realized was that the higher interest rates on these junk bonds more than made up for the increased likelihood of default. In fact, in most cases, these poorly rated companies still had factories, supply chains, and customers in place. They didn't want to default on their debts any more than their highly-rated peers. The money these companies raised from selling bonds was helping them get back on track. They just needed a bit more time. The key, from an investor standpoint, was to buy the bonds in large enough numbers that if a few companies did default on their debts it wouldn't bring down the entire portfolio. That's what Milken discovered by reading the work of W. Braddock Hickman.

This single insight was worth over $1.3 billion to Drexel during the course of Milken's career there. Milken and his team created an entirely new market and they pioneered an approach that to this day makes capital available to companies who don't have stellar credit. Milken's high-yield bonds, which soon came to be known as "junk bonds," have helped thousands of companies stay in business during tough times. They've also made billions in passive income for investors all over the world.

However, Milken's story doesn't end there. A few years later, in 1989, he was busted for fraud and insider trading by the Securities and Exchange Commission and ordered to pay a fine of $600 million and serve 10 years in prison. He ended up being released after just 20 months, but he's now banned from working in the financial securities industry in any capacity for the rest of his life. Today, the 73-year-old Milken is worth $3.7 billion and he runs a charity focused on raising money to fund prostate cancer research. Some people love him while others hate him. However, he's still eerily well-respected on Wall Street.

I'm not here to debate about whether Milken was right or wrong. The important point to remember from his story is that fixed income investments can be extremely powerful, but they are often overlooked. Bonds, T-Bills, and mortgage-backed securities aren't something you can afford to ignore as you seek to build passive income for yourself. As Milken demonstrated, it's possible to make significant money investing in fixed-income securities...if you know what you're doing.

Don't Write Off This Simple Investing Trick

Fixed income securities have gotten a bad reputation and they have significant limitations compared to other types of investments, but I have a few tips and tricks for how to put this passive income vehicle to work for you in a way that makes sense. I'll show you how to take advantage of the benefits of this asset class, like low risk and high liquidity, while avoiding the disadvantages. But first, why are these securities scoffed at by so many investors?

The first reason most investors aren't excited about fixed income securities is that they promise only small returns. As I write this, the current interest rate for a 52-week U.S. Treasury Bill is just .16%. That means you could buy a $1,000 T-Bill, wait an entire year for it to mature, and you'll only make $1.60. This doesn't exactly sound like a get-rich-quick scheme. Actually, with the inflation rate currently hovering around 2%, you would be losing about $14-$15 during the next year by investing in a T-Bill right now.

Another worrisome thing about fixed income securities, like T-Bills, is the possibility of getting "locked up" at a low-interest rate. Accountants call this "interest rate risk." For instance, if you spent your last $1,000 to buy a 52-week T-Bill today at .16% and then the rate shot up to 2.75% next month, you wouldn't be able to buy a new bill and take advantage of the higher rate. You would still be locked in at the lower rate for eleven more months until your bill matures. You could try to sell off your old bill and buy a new one. However, with the new "going rate" of 2.75% it might be hard to find a buyer for your .16% T-Bill unless you offer a discount. By the time you do that, you may be better off just holding onto it yourself.

Finally, one of the biggest reasons why many investors today are wary of fixed income securities is they can be defaulted on. If the issuer of your bond defaults, you'll lose your principal and you'll stop receiving coupon payments. This means it's possible to purchase a bond and later receive nothing back at all. If the company that issued your bond goes bankrupt, they won't be able to pay you anymore. You'll get nothing. Therefore, fixed-income investments have no low end. The issuer can file for bankruptcy and default on their entire debt to you.

Conversely, there is a firm high-end limit on all fixed-income investments. No matter how well a company performs, they will never pay you a cent more than they promised. No matter how well the U.S. economy does, you won't earn any extra money from the U.S. government when you cash in your T-Bill. You'll receive the exact amount that was promised when you purchased it, that's the best-case scenario.

This means there is an imbalance. There's a firm high-end limit but no low end at all.

In the investing world, the chance to make an extremely high amount of money on an investment is referred to as "upside." For example, investing in Google at their IPO and seeing your money multiply by over 1,000% would represent a huge upside. Fixed income investments, on the other hand, don't have any kind of upside. With a bond or a T-Bill, you're never going to be surprised and wind up making a killing. You're always going to get exactly what you were promised—or maybe less.

The idea in investing is generally to maximize your profit while minimizing the risk of losing your money. But, by definition, the more a bond is paying you, the worse it will be rated. This means in order to receive high coupon payments on a fixed income investment portfolio you have to focus on bonds issued by companies who have lower-than-perfect credit ratings. T-Bills and AAA-rated bonds are just too "safe" to yield impressive returns.

The good news with bonds and other fixed-income investments is that they are often traded on financial markets. Any time assets are traded it means there will be "deals" available. There are always going to be certain securities that are expensive because they are "hot" and in demand. And there will be others trading at a discount because nobody wants them right now. The market prices can fluctuate based on not only actual monetary value, but also on their perceived value to other investors at any given time. And this perceived value is dependent on the opinion of buyers in the market as to whether a company will be able to cover its debts.

In order to make serious money in fixed income securities, you need to locate "good deals." This means you need to somehow be able to see value others don't see. You must identify bonds that are currently trading cheap because other investors don't have much faith in the ability of the companies that issued them to pay back their debts. These can be the most profitable bonds of all, which is what Michael Milken discovered back in the 1960s.

Imagine you recently bought $10,000 worth of bonds from a leading car manufacturer. You might have received a rate of about 4% on this type of bond with a 3-year maturity date. That means you'll earn $40 in coupon payments per year (or $20 every six months) and then you'll receive your original $10,000 back along with the final payment at the end of the three years. However, what would happen if just a few weeks after you purchased your bonds this same auto manufacturer was involved in a major recall? All of a sudden, the media will be running stories about how the manufacturer owes billions to replace thousands of vehicles. Next, there will be a rush of people trying to sell their bonds. At this point, your $10,000 bond might only go for $5,000 or $6,000 on the open market.

When a bond is trading for a discount off its face value like this, it means the market has low confidence in the company's ability to pay back the debt. Securities like this are potentially a highly profitable investment. If you buy up these low-rated bonds and the companies end up paying back their debts, you'll make out exceptionally well. The key is being able to determine which low-rated companies are most likely to pay back their debts successfully. Those are the bonds you want to buy.

Here's a theme you'll see echoed in this book often: good investing is about deep preparation and careful research. Look closer at the Michael Milken story from earlier in the chapter and you'll see he spent years researching securities markets—first at Berkeley, then at Wharton, and finally on the job at Drexel. I had a mentor who taught me how to perform proper research before buying anything.

No matter what types of passive income securities you choose to invest in, this theme is always going to be the same. Never invest in anything before you clearly understand why it's a better investment than something

else you could be buying. Don't buy a company's bonds until you've read their most recent annual report—along with the annual reports of their top five biggest competitors. You can get all of these for free by calling the companies directly and asking them to send you a copy.

What should you look for when you are reading a company's annual report? Ninety percent of the content is fluff that can be ignored. But amidst the fluff there will be a few obvious clues about how the company is doing. The main thing I usually look for is cashflow. If there is revenue coming into a company's books every month, they can usually find a way to pay off their debts. On the other hand, if a company is struggling to bring in enough work to scrape by each month, or if they have been unable to get key products to market, they might not be able to afford to pay off their outstanding bond debt. As you read a company's annual report, pay special attention to their recent cashflow figures. Get a mentor who can help you dig deeper into the reports and understand the numbers. Don't buy anything you don't understand.

There's another type of fixed income asset that captures some upside potential. It's called a convertible bond. In most ways, convertibles function just like standard bonds. You'll receive regular coupon payments for the duration of the bond and on the maturation date you'll get your principal back. The main difference is that with a convertible you'll also have the option to buy a certain number of shares of the company's stock on the maturation date as well. This means if the company performs exceptionally well during the years you're holding the bond, you'll not only benefit by collecting interest payments the entire time, but you'll also be able to turn a profit on your shares in the company. Convertibles are a great way to combine stability and predictability of fixed income with the higher upside potential of the stock market.

The bottom line is that fixed income assets aren't just for your grandparents anymore. There is some real money to be made investing in this sector today, but in my own passive income investing I only use fixed income securities for certain functions. Let's talk about exactly when and how to use these assets for best results.

How to Make Fixed Income Work for You

The reason I say "make fixed income work *for you*" is because there's no such thing as a security that's always a good buy for every investor. The "perfect portfolio" is different for everyone, and it's up to each individual to discover what that looks like to them. But there are some tips that can save you a lot of trial and error.

The main benefits of fixed income are stability, consistency, predictability, and a low level of risk. These investments generate payments on a set schedule and you can be sure you'll get your money on time, exactly as promised, unless there is a bankruptcy. On the other hand, you can expect lower overall returns with fixed-income investments, as well as little to no upside. Because they are far less risky than most other types of assets, fixed income securities don't pay particularly well. And, regardless of how well the issuing entity performs during the time you're holding their bonds, they won't pay you any kind of bonus. This means fixed income securities are a good addition to your portfolio when stability and safety are more important than large gains.

For example, during periods of high market volatility or economic recession when it becomes harder to consistently choose winning investments, you might want to shift more of your portfolio into fixed income securities. Any time there is a high level of uncertainty, markets get riskier. To avoid some of this risk and provide some reliable cashflow, you can take advantage of the steady, predictable, low-risk nature of fixed income assets. Then, when the economic cycle resets and things start to calm down again in the global markets, you can begin to return your capital to other types of securities that have more potential upside.

Another set of factors to consider includes your current career stage, the size of your savings, and your goals for retirement. If you are early in your working life and anticipate earning wages for decades to come, you'll probably want to focus attention on assets with a greater potential upside. Fixed income securities might be too "safe" at this point. However, if you're later in your career or thinking about retiring soon—or if you've already retired—safety and predictability will likely be more important. This is when fixed income starts to make a lot more sense.

Think about your own goals and your current financial situation, including the state of the economy right now. Is stability, predictability, and safety more important, or would you prioritize upside and potential gains more at this moment in time? To help you consider whether fixed income might be right for you as a passive income strategy, here's my "report card." I've graded this asset class in 7 different categories as either "Low," "Moderate," or "High." For each rating, I also provide a small explanation.

Report Card: Fixed Income

Time Commitment: Low

Once purchased, fixed-income assets are entirely passive. There is nothing you have to do in order to receive your payments. In the case of a convertible bond, you'll just have to decide whether you'd like to exercise your stock option or not. That's the only action you need to take. As with any investment, I recommend that you perform thorough research before purchasing any fixed-income assets.

Dealflow: High

The market for fixed income investments is huge as there are always plenty of governments, organizations, and corporations looking to sell off some structured debt. This means you'll never have a shortage of candidates. Depending on market forces, interest rates can fluctuate considerably from week to week. Start paying attention to this. As interest rates rise, fixed-income investments become more attractive.

Capital Commitment: Low

Bonds and T-Bills can be purchased for virtually any amount—as low as $1. This means there isn't a high initial investment required. The financial barrier to entry is extremely low. However, fixed income securities also tend to yield lower returns than other assets. This means it doesn't necessarily make sense to focus on fixed income if you have a low amount of capital to work worth. In that case, you might be better off turning your attention to some of the strategies you'll read about later.

Knowledge Requirement: Low

Fixed income securities can get extremely complicated, and there are people (like Mike Milken) who spend their entire careers immersed in the complexities and subtleties of the bond market. However, for the average middle-of-the-road investor looking to get into fixed income securities, the knowledge requirement isn't steep compared to other assets. Buy a handful of books, take a few online courses, and try to find a mentor to show you the ropes. But don't be shy to jump in and learn as you go.

Return Potential (ROI): Low

Historically, returns on fixed-income investments have been low compared to other asset classes. Because fixed income securities come with an unusually low level of risk, they don't offer a high return on their payments. The exception is low-grade, or junk bonds, which pay a much higher coupon rate than investment-grade bonds, but are also more likely to default. These are the bonds that made Milken his millions back in the 70s and 80s.

Risk Level: Low

Fixed income securities are one of the safest investments in existence. With any investment-grade bonds on the market, your chances of losing money are exceptionally small. Bonds and T-Bills can be counted on. Of course, if you opt for high-yield junk bonds, there will be a moderate level of risk attached. However, as Milken proved, this can be mitigated to some extent by maintaining a diversified portfolio.

Upside: Low

Unless you are trading low-rated junk bonds, there is essentially no upside to be had in fixed-income investments. When a bond matures, your principal is returned and nothing else. One way to add some upside is to look for discounted bonds that are trading below their face value. Another strategy is to look at a security called a convertible bond. This will give you the option when it matures to purchase shares in the company at a past stock price. If it goes up while you hold the bond, you can make significant money.

The Bottom Line

The defining features of fixed-income investments are low risk, predictability, steady income, a low rate of return, and lack of upside. These types of assets make sense when there is uncertainty in the economy or when you are approaching retirement and want to add low-risk passive income to your portfolio. To make real money with fixed income you have to take on some higher-risk "junk" bonds, and this means you'll need to perform careful research to find companies that are going to be able to pay back their debts. It also helps to diversify.

In the next chapter, I'll cover the safest form of passive income on the planet, and I'll show you a trick Benjamin Franklin used to turn $1,000 into over $5 million...

Video Assignment #2: Why Bonds Aren't Always a Safe Bet

This chapter, I'm sharing a video that explores fixed income in the context of our contemporary and future markets. There is increased concern about where the fixed income market is headed in the coming years, particularly after the events of 2020. A safer place to invest away from the future bond market mess is intangible assets that can generate long-term income.

To access the video, go to passiveincomethebook.com/2.

CHAPTER 3

Savings Vehicles

When he died in 1790, the great statesman and inventor Benjamin Franklin left an unusual request in his will, which would take two hundred years and four generations of lawyers to complete. By the time his request was fully executed, it raised millions of dollars to fund public works and entrepreneurship in two major Eastern cities. It would also demonstrate an important lesson about the power of compound interest—only, it wasn't the lesson Franklin had expected to teach.

Ben's dying wish was a financial experiment that involved friendly competition between his two favorite U.S. cities to determine which was a better place to do business. He also wanted to put his wealth to good use in the community. Therefore, as a part of his will, Franklin asked for two separate trust funds to be established in his name, one at a Boston bank and the other at a bank in Philadelphia. Franklin left exactly 1,000 pounds sterling to start each trust (the equivalent of approximately $4,500 today). He specified that the funds were to be loaned out to young men looking to start a business at 5% annual interest.

But even Franklin himself couldn't have predicted what would happen to his trusts over the next 200 years...

The rules set forth in Franklin's will declared that the trusts would be left alone to grow for exactly 100 years. Then, at the end of 100 years, 75% of each account balance would be donated to schools and public works projects. The remaining 25% of each trust would be left for another 100 years to continue growing and being loaned out to young entrepreneurs. Finally, at the end of the second 100-year period, the balance of each trust would be donated to its respective city.

Franklin predicted the trusts would reach over $10 million at the end of the contest. However, his estimates were not even close. By 1990 the Boston trust had reached a value of just $5.5 million and the Philadelphia trust was worth only $2.5 million. As Franklin had wanted, the funds were given to each city to support schools and scholarships. But why did the trusts end up with so much less money than he predicted? And what caused the Boston trust to balloon to more than twice the size of the one in Philadelphia?

It turns out Franklin dramatically overestimated the power of compound interest as a long-term wealth-building tool. A quick look at the history of interest rates will help illustrate where he went wrong.

Anthropologists believe the idea of paying interest on loans is even older than the existence of money itself. The practice is thought to have originated with seed and grain banks in the cities of ancient Mesopotamia, where prehistoric farmers could borrow the seeds and animal feed they needed for a season. In exchange, they were expected to eventually return everything they borrowed, plus interest. Banks used these interest payments to grow their wealth of seeds and feed for the future. This simple economic tool facilitated rapid expansion and the practice proved so successful it has continued in one form or another ever since.

Some of the earliest human texts dating back thousands of years contain references to loans and interest rates. Hammurabi's code, for example, written around 1750 BCE, decreed that all loans should be paid back with a 20% interest rate. The economic texts of ancient Rome and

Greece suggest interest rates fluctuated between about 5-15% at different times. In the middle ages interest was banned altogether. "Usury," or profiting off a loan, was considered a sin in Abrahamic traditions. By the 14th century, however, interest was back in style within the banking systems of the Italian renaissance. In 1420 the Florentine government imposed an interest rate ceiling of 20%. Over the years, interest rates have fluctuated wildly up and down. Today, the U.S. federal interest rate is just .16%, which is extraordinarily low.

When Franklin made his careful calculations back in the 1780s, he never could have imagined that interest rates would drop so precipitously in the coming centuries. He assumed his trusts would continue to generate around 5% per year for their 200-year lifetimes. However, in truth, the average interest rate during those two centuries was significantly less than 5%. In Philadelphia the rates tended to run just a hair lower than they did in Boston, and over the course of 200 years these minuscule differences added up to a large overall gap.

There are two important morals to learn from Franklin's story. First, you have no control over interest rates and they shouldn't be counted on. Never assume you will be able to maintain a certain rate of return on your money. You never know what interest rates are going to do in the future. Second, even miniscule differences in interest rates can add up to a big change over time. It's worth it to put in some effort to make sure you're earning the highest possible amount of interest you can on your money.

Just like fixed income, savings vehicles are very safe. In fact, all U.S. savings accounts are insured by the federal government for up to $250,000. So even if your bank goes out of business and is unable to return your money, you'll still get it back. All of this safety and predictability means you shouldn't expect huge returns.

The important benefit of savings vehicles is liquidity. Your funds will be immediately available for withdrawal or transfer any time you want (though you'll be limited to six withdrawals per month with a classic savings account). This is different from a corporate bond or T-Bill, where you can't get your money back until the maturation date is reached. With a savings account, the bank will loan your money out to other customers in order to earn interest, but you'll still be able to withdraw it whenever you like.

There are a few different types of savings vehicles offered by banks and credit unions today. The most popular types of interest-bearing accounts are savings accounts, certificates of deposit (CDs), and money market accounts. Each has its own privileges and restrictions.

The first type of savings vehicle is a standard savings account. These are offered by banks and can provide a wide range of different levels of return. Currently, most banks offer low rates of return, but more competitive rates can be found with some research. One big benefit of savings accounts is that you don't need much money to open one. Some banks have minimum account balances, but typically these aren't unreasonable. Be aware of any requirements when you sign up. The biggest fee to worry about with a savings account comes from making withdrawals too often. Federal law requires that the frequency of withdrawals or purchases from savings accounts does not exceed six per monthly statement cycle.

Another type of savings vehicle is called a certificate of deposit (CD). These generally require more capital than a savings account to start. You can purchase a CD for $500 or $1000 on the low end, and up to $25,000 on the high end. Like a savings account, a CD will generate payments at a fixed interest rate. However, unlike a savings account, with a CD your funds will be less liquid. You can't easily adjust your balance six times each month in a CD account like you can with a savings account. You can't make additional deposits or withdrawals. Once you invest in a CD you shouldn't touch the money until its maturity date unless you want to incur a substantial fee.

The length of time you'll have to wait for your CD to come to maturation varies widely, from around six months to 5-7 years or more. Generally, the longer you invest for, the better your rate will be. And this rate is locked, fixed, and reliable. It isn't subject to change with market fluctuations, like savings accounts. It's incredibly stable, promising a non-volatile, guaranteed return.

A third type of savings vehicle is called a Money Market account. This functions much like a standard savings account. You can deposit money any time you want. You'll be limited to six withdrawals per month. You'll have a minimum balance to maintain. And you'll earn interest each month. However, with a Money Market account your money will be invested into CDs and financial markets, not lent out to other individuals. You'll also be able to write checks and to access your money via ATMs, which you can't do using a standard savings account.

You're likely to see money market accounts pay a higher interest rate than regular savings accounts. However, they generally boast a heftier minimum balance requirement as well. Also, it's worth noting that interest rates are variable and are dependent on market conditions with a money market account, whereas a CD locks in one guaranteed rate until the security matures.

As Franklin's 200-year experiment proved, you probably aren't going to get rich using a savings account (at least, not in a single lifetime). However, when used properly, these assets can absolutely make a difference in your bottom line. Let's explore how you can do it right.

Get Advanced with Your Savings Plan

Savings vehicles are one of the most basic and straightforward types of passive investments, but there are also some advanced-level tactics used by savvy investors to take their savings game to the next level. The main thing to keep track of in the world of savings vehicles is the *federal funds rate*. This serves as a benchmark for how much interest banks can charge on loans. When the federal funds rate drops, it means banks can borrow money from each other without paying much interest. On the other hand, a high federal funds rate means banks face steep interest fees in order to borrow money. In response, the banks will usually start to pay consumers more competitive interest rates to attract deposits.

With any type of savings vehicle your money is going to be gaining interest at a slow-and-steady rate from your financial institution. Anything up to $250,000 per account is insured by the U.S. federal government and is therefore secure. The interest rate will fluctuate up and down to reflect the strength of the economy.

When interest rates are high, it generally means people are making money with confidence and the economy is thriving. Whereas low rates usually reflect a period of economic stagnation. Historically, the federal reserve bank has used low rates as a way to make it cheaper for financial institutions and businesses to borrow money, stimulating the economy.

As I write this book, interest rates are at an all-time low, at less than 1% for a majority of interest-bearing accounts. This is not just a 10-year or 20-year low. This isn't even a low for the past century. Today's interest rates are more like a 5000-year low. You would have made significantly more passive income loaning seeds to farmers in ancient Mesopotamia than you can by investing in a savings account today.

I encourage all serious investors to take note of the federal funds rate at least once per week. This isn't something to obsess about, but it's a good habit to be in and it can make you a lot of money over the course of your investing life. Ask yourself these questions each week:

1. What is the current interest rate?
2. Is it high or low?
3. Do experts think it's heading up or down in the coming weeks?

In the leadup to the 2008 financial crash the federal interest had been climbing steadily to the point where it surpassed 5%. As soon as the economy started to tank, the Federal Reserve immediately stepped in to bring down the interest rate, making capital more easily available and stimulating the economy.

More recently, in the wake of the Covid-19 outbreak, the same pattern played out once again. The federal funds rate had been creeping upward since 2008 and was almost up to 2.5% by February 2020. But as soon as the economy started to experience turbulence in March, the Federal Reserve reduced the rate to nearly zero. If you're serious about learning how to build passive income, the interest rate is something you should be informed about.

When you understand the federal funds rate, you can begin to get more advanced with your savings plan. Different types of savings vehicles turn out to be better deals depending on whether current interest rates are high or low. Instead of holding all of your savings in the same account, it might make sense to split it up in different ways at different times. Depending on current interest rates, you can shift your money between standard savings accounts, money market funds, and certificates of deposit (CDs).

If the funds rate is low and you think it might increase soon, you'll want to avoid CDs because these savings vehicles lock you into the current interest rate until their maturation date. It doesn't make sense to lock yourself into an exceptionally low rate for an extended period of time. However, if the funds rate is low and is expected to stay low for a long time—or to drop further—it might make sense to grab a few CDs because you can usually get a better rate on these than you can with a savings account.

During times when the federal funds rate is high, by contrast, it definitely makes sense to buy CDs and lock in the high rate. This is especially true when it is anticipated that interest rates will drop again in the near future. If you would have purchased some CDs when the funds rate was

5% back in 2007, you would still be getting paid at the 5% even though the new rate is 0.16%. Because CDs are less liquid, you'll probably want to hold back some cash in a money market account so you can purchase more CDs if interest rates climb higher.

With CDs, every small change in the interest rate matters—a lot. When you can't touch your money for 5 years, even a fraction of a percent can make a big difference. This means you really don't want to get locked up in low-performing CDs. One strategy used by many investors is to purchase multiple CDs that all have different maturation dates. This way, when the shorter-term CDs mature, you can either use the money to reinvest in new CDs if the interest rate has gone up, or you can switch it over to a money market account if the federal funds rate has dropped. By spreading out your initial investment over a range of different maturation periods, you can protect yourself against rapid changes in interest rates.

Another practice recommended by some investing experts is to open a new 12-month CD every month. With this strategy, you won't get any money back for the first year, but once you make it to the second year you'll start to see returns every single month, which you can reinvest in a new CD. This way, you'll generate some passive income that is steady and reliable, and after a few years you'll have a full year's worth of monthly income tucked away for a rainy day. Also, you'll be able to take advantage of the fact that CDs pay a higher interest rate than savings accounts.

In order to pull off this monthly CD strategy, known as a "CD Ladder," you'll want to save up a full year's worth of expenses because you won't be able to access the savings until each CD matures. If you can pull this off, it's a great feeling to know you have a year of monthly income stacked up and ready. And with the CD Ladder approach, you'll be earning decent returns the whole way.

As your ladder grows each year, you might choose to invest your extra monthly earnings into a longer-term CD with a higher rate. Soon, you'll be investing in a five-year CD every month on top of your one-year CD. The longer certificates will earn an even better return every year. Or you might want to shift your focus to other more lucrative types of passive income investments once you have a year's worth of CD income. For instance, you could start buying bonds to save up for a larger real estate investment. Or you could invest in a private equity fund or venture capital fund. I'll cover each of those options in later chapters.

A final thought to consider on money market, savings, and CD accounts: they help you spend less money. Since each type of account has its own limits on the number of transactions you're allowed to make, you might find yourself naturally dipping in less frequently. This of course will help your money grow bigger faster. CDs, specifically, are great savings vehicles because you have to buy them up front and can't touch your money until they mature. You won't be tempted to dig in because you'll know your money is tied up. And you can always rest assured knowing you're getting a great interest rate compared to a typical savings account or money market fund.

I use these types of assets all the time. Now, let's break down how this approach could fit into your overall passive income strategy.

Use Savings Vehicles to Build Passive Income

Most personal finance experts recommend saving up anywhere from a few months' to a year's-worth of living costs in an emergency fund. This way you'll be prepared for surprise expenses like injury, illness, home repair, or job loss when they spring up. According to a recent poll, more than a third of American households would be plunged into financial hardship if they were faced with an unexpected charge for just $400. Millions live paycheck to paycheck. When a black swan like Covid-19 comes along, we suddenly have half the country enrolling in unemployment.

I don't know about you, but I'd rather not spend my days in fear of financial disaster. I want the safety, security, and confidence of knowing I have enough savings to weather any storm life throws at me—I want a "rainy day" fund.

By definition your rainy day fund, or emergency fund, should be kept highly accessible. After all, what good is it if you can't easily use the money in case of an unexpected event? This means you don't want to purchase stocks, bonds, or real estate with the money in your emergency fund. Your rainy day account shouldn't be invested in anything that needs to be sold before you can spend the cash. Instead, you'll want to maintain your rainy day fund in a liquid form. The three savings vehicles—savings accounts, CDs, and Money Market accounts—are a perfect way to accomplish this.

How does a savings account compare to a standard checking account? A checking account is certainly easier and saves time. But let's do some math. The average Baby Boomer who is close to retirement makes $57,000 per year. That means if you follow my recommendation to save up six months' worth of income, you might be carrying around about $28,500 in your emergency fund at all times. Even if you only go for half my recommendation, you'll still have $14,250 saved up. If your income is higher, or if you decide to go for a full year of savings, you might have much more than this. When you consider that this money will be sitting in savings for the rest of your life, the small difference in interest rates between a checking account and a Money Market savings account adds up to a lot. It makes sense to maintain your emergency fund in an interest-bearing account.

Ben Franklin's trust fund experiment showed that minor, seemingly insignificant fluctuations in the interest rate can make a substantial difference over time in the balance of a fund. At the end of 200 years, one of Ben's trusts was more than twice the size of the other. In the same way, because you'll be holding onto your emergency fund for many years, and because it will contain thousands of dollars, small differences in the interest rate will make a big difference in the balance over the long term. Don't maintain this fund in a checking account. If you do, you'll be missing out on years' worth of potential gains. A savings account or Money Market account would make the most sense. The interest you earn will add up to thousands of dollars during your life. Do the research.

Of course, interest-bearing accounts aren't only for rainy day funds. You can use these types of accounts any time you're holding a decent amount of money in one place and you need to keep it liquid and available. For instance, if you're saving up for a down payment on a house or a new car, a Money Market account is a great place to do so. You might even want to open a separate account for each savings project that you're working on. For instance, you can have one account for your rainy day fund, another for your mortgage down payment, and a third for your next car.

The annual inflation rate of 2% means that next year a $100 bill will only buy you $98 worth of stuff by today's standards. For every dollar you leave sitting around, you are actually losing a couple pennies in purchasing power each year. One of the simplest ways to stop losing money is to open a high-yield savings account for your rainy day fund, mortgage payments, and any other big savings projects.

Report Card: Savings / CDs / Money Market

Time Commitment: Low

Investing in interest-bearing accounts takes little effort. The most you'll have to do is some quick research to find the best rates (particularly for CDs) and then you can take a step back and let the cash flow in. As far as maintaining your accounts, you should be diligent about keeping an eye on federal funds rates so you can know if your investments need to be shifted around.

Dealflow: High

The deal flow for these accounts is excellent as there will always be financial institutions offering money market, savings, and CD accounts. You'll constantly have dozens of different offers to consider. Again, interest rates fluctuate rapidly so it's important to follow the federal funds rate to know the ideal time to make changes to your accounts.

Capital Commitment: Low

These types of accounts require a low amount of capital to get started. They are designed to be accessible to all people. Since banks generally want more people to open accounts (especially when the fed fund rate is high) there are low minimum requirements to get started. Savings accounts and CDs require anywhere from a few hundred dollars to $1000 as a minimum investment, depending on the account. Money market accounts are the most expensive to open and generally require at least a $2,500 balance to avoid incurring fees.

Knowledge Requirement: Low

The base knowledge necessary to be successful with this type of asset is low. Looking at the history of interest rates over the last few decades is really all you need to do in order to be informed about whether any specific interest-bearing account is a good investment in the present. Since changes in interest rates are predictable, you can rely on a few patterns to inform whether or not you should invest.

Return Potential (ROI): Low

Unless your name is Benjamin Franklin and you're opening an account that will compound every year for 200 years, you probably aren't going to make a fortune with a savings account. It's true there were times when interest rates could really work for you and turn a decent profit, but that isn't the case today. It could be decades before interest rates return to a level that would make these accounts more viable as an investing strategy. Or maybe they never will.

Risk Level: Low

Interest-bearing accounts backed by the FDIC are extremely secure. You might not keep up with inflation on every account you open, but there is virtually no risk you will lose money. Even in a doomsday scenario, when your bank goes out of business and can't afford to pay you back, your accounts are insured up to $250,000 per account. If you need to put some money away for the long-term, or just need a rainy day fund, savings accounts, CDs, and money market accounts are some of the most reliable places on the planet to park your cash.

Upside: Low

The upside on these accounts is practically nonexistent. The money you put in is the same as the money you'll get out, plus a few cents in interest. In the case of some CDs, you might be offered a rising rate, which means you'll have the option to increase the interest rate to match a new offer. You can usually only do this once or twice before the CD matures. In this way, you might get a little bit more money back than you initially planned. However, that's hardly an upside in the typical sense of the word.

The Bottom Line

These accounts are great to save for big-ticket purchases or to protect yourself from an emergency situation. The interest rates offered are not significant, but what they lack in profitability, they make up for in security. You won't lose anything by investing in CDs, savings, or money market accounts. Every investor should use these instruments for readily-available capital. For the greatest return on your rainy-day fund, a CD ladder might be your best bet, in which investments are staggered out in time. But today's historically low interest rates make interest-bearing accounts a poor choice for generating passive income.

While savings vehicles aren't exactly going to make you a millionaire by themselves, the passive income strategy I'm going to cover in the next chapter definitely can: dividend stocks.

Video Assignment #3: Understanding the Kiddie Tax

This chapter, we explored savings vehicles. While I generally believe the ROI from savings accounts is minimal, I do think they can be useful as an emergency fund, especially if you have a family.

What's another way to save a little money for your family? Through taxes. You can save your family $1,642.83 per year in taxes by taking advantage of a recent loophole in the tax code, known as the Kiddie Tax. By allocating some of your investment income to your children, you can even pay for their college education.

To access the video, go to passiveincomethebook.com/3.

CHAPTER 4

Dividend Stocks

The death of Ronald Read in 2015 at the age of 92 sent shockwaves through the city of Brattleboro, Vermont. This friendly local janitor was well-known around town for pinching his pennies. He drove a used Toyota Yaris and wasn't afraid to walk many blocks to avoid paying a parking meter. For years he used safety pins to button his jacket together after the zipper broke. He even chopped his own firewood in his 90s to save a few dollars on the heating bill.

But Ronald Read had a secret that not even his closest friends or family members knew about: he was worth $7.9 million.

"He was a hard worker," said Read's stepson, Phillip Brown, after his death, "but I don't think anybody had an idea that he was a multimillionaire." The news of the vast fortune he'd accumulated caught everyone who knew Read completely by surprise. As a janitor at the nearby JCPenney, his salary had been just $25,000 per year. How did a man with no finance training and such a modest income manage to build so much wealth?

It turns out Read had a secret safety deposit box at the local bank that he didn't tell anyone about. The lockbox did not contain old family gemstones, gold bars, or priceless antique pistols. Instead, it was full of stock certificates. When the certificates were compiled and organized, the full stack of 95 certificates was over five inches tall. Read had been slowly and steadily buying stocks for his entire life and never sold any. Most certificates were decades old. But the interesting thing about Read's paper portfolio was not how old or how many certificates he had: it was which stocks Read had picked. The 95 companies that Read owned shares in turned out to be excellent choices. His savvy investing had made him very wealthy. So how did he choose his stocks?

According to those who knew him, Read was a daily reader of *The Wall Street Journal*. But he didn't load his portfolio with the flashy new tech companies that often grab *Wall Street Journal* headlines. He didn't own any Facebook or Twitter. He wasn't investing in biotech or fintech. In fact, his portfolio seems rather ordinary and boring at first glance. You have to look deeper to see Read's true investing genius.

The companies Read bought shares in were spread across many industries and business models, but they all had one main thing in common: dividends. He focused on stocks that pay regular dividends to their shareholders every quarter. This allowed Read to build up a massive amount of passive income. When he died, Read was earning $20,000 per month in dividend payments from his portfolio alone. That's over $240,000 in annual passive income.

A dividend payment is a way for companies to share profits with shareholders. When a publicly traded company makes money, they have two basic options for what to do with it. They can either reinvest the profits to grow the company or they can return the profits to shareholders. When a company is young and has a lot of growth potential, it makes sense to invest all or most of their profits in growth. But when a company becomes more mature and reaches the point where they dominate a market, growth will inevitably slow. In this case, investing in growth will yield diminishing returns and it may make more sense to return a share of profits directly to shareholders.

The Coca-Cola Company, for example, was founded on January 29, 1892, in Atlanta, Georgia. For the first seventy-two years the company was in business, they paid no dividend whatsoever to their shareholders. It made more sense to invest every possible dollar in growing the company. Then, in 1964, the company introduced a small dividend of one cent per share. In the decades since, the dividend has increased each year. Today, Coca-Cola's dividend sits around $1.60 per share.

In general, a company does not offer dividends until it is well-established and completely dominates a market. That's part of the reason why Ronald Read's portfolio was so boring. It was full of old, well-respected companies like Wells Fargo, Procter & Gamble, Colgate-Palmolive, American Express, and Johnson & Johnson because those are the ones with a strong history of dividends.

The downside of focusing only on dividend-paying stocks, as Read did, is that they don't have a lot of growth potential. In general, these stocks aren't going to surprise you with a huge surge in value. That's why they are offering dividends. When continued growth is no longer guaranteed, companies shift toward dividends as a way to keep investors interested.

There is less upside in dividend stocks than there is in growth stocks. For Read, the lack of upside wasn't a problem. He wasn't looking to buy and sell. He was in it for the long haul with his investments. In fact, his antique method of using actual physical certificates for all of his holdings meant in order to sell a stock he had to actually drive to the bank, open his safety deposit box, find the certificate in his 5-inch stack, drive to his brokerage, and fill out all kinds of paperwork. That's why he never sold anything.

By using a trading method that made it difficult for him to sell his stocks, Read forced himself to hold onto them even when the companies went through hard times. This allowed him to reap massive returns when most of them eventually rebounded.

But if Read was making $20,000 in passive income each month when he died, why was he still buttoning his coat with safety pins and walking blocks to avoid parking meters? And why on Earth was he still working as a janitor at JCPenney for $25,000 per year when he was worth $7.9 million?

Read wasn't touching the dividends generated by his portfolio because he was re-investing them all back into more shares of stock. That's what allowed him to make such incredible gains. Even just in the last decade, studies show that people who re-invested their dividends earned 2% higher returns than those who opted to be paid out. That's the difference between 8% and 6% overall returns. In the long run, that's a huge amount.

Re-investing is the secret that helped push Read's portfolio up to $7.9 million. Each quarter, he re-invested the dividend payments from his stocks and used them to buy even more shares. This created an exponential cumulative effect over time. He held down his job as a janitor so that he would be able to keep re-investing his dividends and he would never have to dip into his investment income to pay his living expenses.

When Read died, he left $4.8 million to Battleboro Memorial Hospital. He'd been a regular there for many years, not as a patient but at the hospital cafe. "He always had a cup of coffee and an English muffin with peanut butter," said Ellen Smith, a server at the cafe. "That was it. And he always sat at the exact same stool on the counter."

He also left $1.2 million to Brooks Memorial Library, where he was a frequent patron. These were the largest donations the hospital or library had ever received. In fact, the library only had a $600,000 budget for their entire year.

"It was a thunderbolt from the sky," said the library's executive director, Jerry Carbone.

"It was the talk of the town," said library director Starr LaTronica a year after Read's death. "People still come in and ask me about it and reference it."

There are many lessons to learn from Read's life. One is the beauty of extreme generosity. Another is the benefit of thrift and saving your money well. Even though he didn't earn a lot, Read was able to save because he was frugal. This shows that anyone can become wealthy if they make good financial decisions daily for years. Another important point is that Read lived to the ripe age of 92, so he had many years to let his money work for him.

Read was able to save $8 million over the course of his life by investing in dividend-producing stocks. He used these assets to slowly build passive income. And he re-invested the income to purchase even more stocks. Over time, this simple strategy yielded impressive results. And it can work for you too. Next, I'm going to explain everything you need to know about how dividends work, when to buy them, and how to choose the right ones.

How to Pick a Winning Dividend Stock

Here's a brilliant get-rich-quick scheme for you: buy a stock on the day before they award their dividend and then sell it the next day, once the dividends have been awarded. You can collect your dividend payment without holding the stock for more than 24 hours. Just flip the stock and cash your dividend check! What could go wrong?

I'm kidding.

This "brilliant" plan is actually a rehashing of an old idea known as "dividend capturing," and it's been debunked. It won't work in the real world for a few reasons. First, as soon as the company pays its dividend the stock price will instantly drop by the same amount because it will be perceived as having that much less value. This means by the time you turn around and try to sell the stock the next day the payment of the dividend will already be reflected in the stock's ticker price. The instant the market opens the stock will already be trading without its dividend and will, therefore, sell for a lower price. You can't possibly sell it fast enough.

The first day after a company pays its dividend is known as the "ex-dividend date," or "ex-date." This is the day the stock begins to trade without its dividend attached. In other words, buy the stock before the ex-date and you'll get the dividend. Buy on or after the ex-date and the previous owner will get it. About two weeks after the ex-date is the pay date, when the payment will actually show up in your brokerage account. In general, the value of the stock drops on the ex-date by approximately the amount of the dividend. That's one reason dividend capturing doesn't work.

Another problem with the dividend capturing approach is that the tax code is specifically designed to penalize investors who hold stocks for a short period of time and then sell. The Securities and Exchange Commission distinguishes between "qualified" and "nonqualified" dividends. Qualified dividends are taxed at the lower *capital gains* rate, whereas nonqualified dividends are taxed at the higher *personal income* rate. When you've held a stock for fewer than 60 days during the 120-day period prior to the ex-date your dividend is considered nonqualified. On the other hand, when you've held it for at least 60 days out of that period the dividend becomes qualified. So even if you do succeed somehow and capture dividends then sell your stock immediately, you'll be placing any earnings you do make directly into the highest tax bracket.

With the dividend capturing approach, you also miss out on the upside potential of dividend stocks. Compared to the first two securities (bonds and savings accounts), dividend stocks have a much larger upside because in addition to the regular quarterly profit distributions they can also appreciate in value significantly.

In order to realize this upside, you have to hold the stocks for many years. That was one of the big lessons from Ronald Read, the $8-million janitor. He kept his stocks in certificate form and never sold any of them. And at the time of his death, some of his holdings had increased in value by four or five times and a few had increased beyond that.

The final issue with the dividend capturing approach, at least from my perspective, is it's not really passive. It requires you to buy and sell a security every time you want to get paid. I believe it's crucial to focus on building income streams that are entirely 100% passive. Otherwise, at the end of the day, you're just creating another job for yourself. Capturing dividends will just become another way of trading your time for money. This is crazy to me because dividends are entirely passive if you just leave them alone and do nothing! In the long run, this works much better than trying to pull off a get-rich-quick scheme with capturing stock dividends.

Do a careful analysis, buy your stocks, hold onto them, and re-invest your checks in more shares. That's the formula that works long-term. It might not be glamorous, but it's effective.

When you're analyzing a dividend stock, the first thing to look at is the yield. This number tells you how high the actual dividend payments are relative to your investment. To calculate it, simply multiply the most recent dividend payment by the total number of payments per year. Finally, divide the that by the company's current stock price and multiply the product by 100%.

For instance, Coca-Cola shares currently pay a cash dividend of $.40 per quarter. That might not sound like much—or maybe it sounds like a great deal—but let's do a little math and calculate the actual yield this number represents. First, multiply $.40 by four, since shareholders will receive four payments per year. This calculation reveals that Coca-Cola pays a total annual dividend of $1.60 per share. Next, divide that by the current share price, which is $55 as I write this, and multiply the final answer by 100%. This gives you a dividend yield of 2.9%. In other words, every dollar you invest in Coca-Cola today will payout 2.9% in dividends each year.

It might seem counterintuitive, but when the price of a stock increases the yield actually decreases. For instance, if the market value of Coca-Cola goes up to $65 next month, the yield will drop to 2.5%. This means as the price of a stock drops, the yield will actually go up. In other words, it's a good deal to buy stocks that are trading for a low amount right now. During the Great Depression, for example, some dividend yields were extremely high simply because market prices were so low. If you're looking for high-yield dividends, you might focus on stocks that are currently trading cheap.

However, a stock's yield is by no means the only thing you should look at before deciding whether or not to buy shares. Before you invest, you always want to make sure the stock isn't a "dividend trap". This is a term for a company offering a dividend that's too high to be sustainable. If you see a yield that is too high—maybe something above 8% or 10%—be cautious. This is getting into the too-good-to-be-true territory. A company offering high-yield dividends may be trying too hard to win over potential investors. Or maybe they are just trading for a really low price right now and you found a great deal. It's important to do thorough research and be positive.

Before you buy a dividend stock you want to make sure they will be able to maintain their dividend for a long time. You could look at the company's most recent reported earnings as one indicator. However, that number can actually be misleading because it often reflects things like depreciation that have nothing to do with how much actual cash a company earned during the quarter. The cash flow statement is usually a better true indicator of whether or not a company will be able to keep paying their dividend going forward. Look for this number on a company's annual or quarterly reports.

The payout ratio is another variable that dividend investors look at as a signal of whether a certain dividend stock is a safe long-term bet. This number is calculated by dividing the dividend by the company's earnings per share. A lower ratio is always better, indicating a higher ability to continue paying the dividend. Anything over 100% is considered a sign of potential trouble. Of course, earnings aren't as good of an indicator as cashflow, but nonetheless this number can still be helpful at a glance.

One more indicator to look at is a company's dividend history. There are various public indices that track which companies have paid dividends consistently and which haven't. For instance, "Dividend Kings" are companies that have increased their dividends for at least fifty straight years. Similarly, "Dividend Aristocrats" have demonstrated at least twenty-five consecutive years of increases to their dividends. Then there are "Dividend Achievers" (10+ years of increases) and "Dividend Contenders" (5-9 years of increases).

Behavioral research has shown that past behavior is one of the best predictors of future behavior. If you're looking for companies that will likely increase their dividend next year, these lists are probably great places to start. Of course, "past results don't guarantee future results," but chances are definitely good that any company that has consistently raised their dividend for fifty straight years will probably continue to do so.

The last thing worth considering is that in order to return profits to shareholders some companies buy back shares of their own stock. This is another way to distribute value to shareholders without actually passing out cash directly. When shares are repurchased, it increases earnings per share, which is a key metric of success for companies. This, in turn, can drive the share price even higher. Another benefit is that with every share the company buys back each outstanding share starts to represent a larger stake of ownership in the company. Often buybacks can actually be a better deal for shareholders in the long run than a cash dividend.

Avoiding Taxes On Your Passive Income

I respect Ronald immensely and I think he was a hero to leave millions to charity in his will. However, I don't recommend other investors focus solely on dividends like he did. Yes, dividend stocks definitely have a place in a healthy passive income portfolio. But they should not be the only asset you buy. Let's look at when dividend stocks make sense and when they don't.

One thing to keep in mind is taxes. Since the money you make from stock dividends is a form of income, it is going to be subject to taxation. Generally, if your dividend income reaches a certain small threshold level in any given year (think: $10 or more), your brokerage will issue a form 1099-DIV, reporting your earnings to the IRS. These gains will then be taxed at a certain rate, depending on your current tax bracket and on whether you're collecting qualified dividends or nonqualified dividends.

It's annoying to be taxed on your own earnings when you're simply planning to re-invest them anyways. And because reinvested dividends account for a substantial portion of stock market returns, these taxes can significantly cut into your long-term upside. Because of this, dividend-bearing stocks are a perfect asset to hold in a tax-free account, like a Roth IRA. With a Roth IRA, you'll be able to invest up to $6,000 per year and you'll keep all of your returns entirely tax-free. These accounts are designed to build wealth for retirement, so if you want to take money out for expenses before your sixty-fifth birthday you will be penalized.

Roth IRAs are a fantastic deal. All returns you make are completely tax-free, which can save you thousands over your lifetime. It makes sense to open one immediately if you haven't already done so, and start saving the maximum $6,000 per year in it. With the money in your Roth IRA, dividend stocks are one of the best things you can invest in.

Many financial advisors will recommend an index fund for your IRA, however, these hardly pay anything in the way of dividends. The overall value of your portfolio might increase with an index fund at an average rate of about 7% per year, but your passive income won't increase at all. And the bigger problem with index funds involves the idea of diversification. Index funds work by spreading your money across a highly diversified sample of stocks. However, some of the all-time best investors and top financial thinkers have explicitly warned against diversifying your portfolio too much:

1. "Sweet are the uses of diversity," noted Adam Smith, "but only if you want to end up in the middle of an average."
2. "If you can identify six wonderful businesses," said Warren Buffett, "that is all the diversification you need."
3. "Put all your eggs in one basket," wrote Mark Twain and Andrew Carnegie, "and WATCH THAT BASKET!"

Instead of spreading your money across thousands of stocks, as is done in an index fund, you'll do better if you focus on just a few stocks that turn out to be good picks. And if you focus on dividend stocks, and re-invest your returns, you'll be building passive income in your IRA in addition to beating that 7% average return in the long run.

When you follow my advice and invest in dividend-bearing stocks with your Roth IRA, you'll be accumulating cash every quarter completely tax-free and you can re-invest that cash in additional shares of dividend-bearing stock. Then, when you turn sixty-five, you can start to live off those dividend payments completely tax-free. It's a great deal. Take advantage of a Roth IRA and start building passive income with dividend stocks. It's one of the best ways to do so.

Report Card: Dividend Stocks

Time Commitment: Moderate

As with any financial asset, do your research before investing in dividend stocks. Look at the cash flow statement, payout ratio, and dividend history to verify that the company has a high probability of continuing their dividend for the foreseeable future. Also, as you receive dividend payments each quarter from your portfolio holdings, you'll want to manually re-invest them in whichever stocks are currently the best deal. This means conducting a new research and re-allocation process every 2-3 months.

Dealflow: High

Dividends are everywhere in the stock market, especially when you look at the oldest, most well-established companies. For instance, roughly eighty percent of all companies in the S&P 500 currently pay a dividend. On the other hand, very few growth stocks do. There are thousands of securities on the market at any time that offer dividend payments if you know where to look. Because there are so many options, I recommend focusing on companies with an established history of maintaining or increasing their dividends.

Capital Commitment: Low

You can invest in a dividend-bearing security for as little as the price of a single share of stock. Depending on the company, this might range from a few dollars to a few hundred dollars. Today, you can even get free trades with many online accounts. The amount of capital required to start buying dividend stocks is extremely low. That's what allowed a low-paid janitor from Battleboro, Vermont, named Ronald Read, to save up $8 million.

Knowledge Requirement: Moderate

Compared to savings accounts, CDs, and bonds (which I covered in previous chapters), dividend stocks are a bit more involved to invest in. To be successful, you'll need background knowledge on how dividends work and in the fundamentals of each specific company. That means reading their annual and quarterly reports. And, because you'll have to continually reinvest your dividends to see real returns, this will be an ongoing process of researching companies and rebalancing your portfolio.

Return Potential (ROI): Moderate

In mid-2019 the average dividend yield was 1.87%, according to Siblis Research. This means above-average dividends of 4-6% are relatively standard. Plus, these payments are on top of any increase in the value of the stock, which has historically been about 7% per year in the stock market. When you add all of this together, it's not uncommon to make decent returns over time by investing in dividend-bearing securities, holding them for many years, and consistently reinvesting the dividends.

Risk Level: Moderate

Unlike with savings accounts and CDs, your money isn't insured by the federal government when you purchase shares of dividend-bearing stock. In fact, the dividend itself isn't even guaranteed. The company is free to suspend it any time they choose. During the 2008 financial meltdown, for instance, nearly all of the big banks either drastically cut their dividend or just got rid of it entirely. When Covid-19 hit, many companies cut back their dividends again. These payments aren't guaranteed; they can be taken away during difficult economic times.

Upside: Moderate

Unlike the first two asset classes I covered, dividend stocks have upside! Because these securities represent shares in real companies, their value can increase significantly if the companies perform better than expected while you hold the stock. This means you can stand to make a lot of money. However, the types of companies that offer the most appealing dividends are generally large, stable, well-established companies that don't have much growth potential. Don't expect a huge upside from a portfolio of dividend-bearing stocks.

The Bottom Line

Dividend stocks are a great asset for virtually every investor because they pay significantly more than savings accounts and bonds and allow for the potential to see a much larger upside. They are usually offered by old, well-established companies that aren't expected to demonstrate a huge level of growth. But compared to savings accounts and bonds, the upside offered by dividend stocks is significant. The best way to make solid long-term returns with this asset is to consistently reinvest your dividends in more shares of stock. This has been shown to improve returns 2%, on average. The best place to hold your dividend-bearing stocks is a Roth IRA or other tax-free savings account, where the full dividend can be reinvested each year.

But what if you want to get rich and retire before you turn 65? In the next chapter, I'm going to dive into the world of private equity investing. But first, let's look at how one group of investors made $14 billion on a single deal...

Video Assignment #4: Invest Like Warren Buffet

You know who else endorses dividend stocks? Warren Buffet. Buffet has an excellent approach when it comes to building generational wealth. He focuses predominantly on dividend bearing stocks and says he looks for companies so good they could be run by an idiot, because sooner or later they will.

To access the video, go to passiveincomethebook.com/4, enter your email, and click play.

CHAPTER 5

Private Equity

When Blackstone Group purchased Hilton Hotels for $27 billion in 2007, their analysts had no idea the real estate bubble was nearing its apex and was about to burst. Blackstone is a massive private equity firm that was known within the investment community for buying struggling companies off the public market, returning them to profitability, and then selling them for a handsome profit. The Hilton deal looked like a slam dunk because most of the hotel company's assets came in the form of real estate, and the real estate market was on fire. Surely Blackstone would have no trouble fixing up Hilton's financials and turning a nice profit in the process.

Except, a few months later, in 2008, the real estate market took a horrifying nosedive. Falling housing prices wiped out billions of dollars in equity overnight. The foreclosure rate came to a boil, doubling in less than a year. It was clear investors with a large portion of their portfolios in real estate would be hit the hardest. Suddenly, Blackstone realized they had chosen a completely inopportune moment to enter into one of the largest private equity deals of all-time. Their $27 billion investment was vanishing before their eyes.

To make matters worse, banks and financial firms were going bankrupt and capital was drying up. Soon after the acquisition, a few of Blackstone's biggest partners in the deal went out of business, including Bear Stearns and Lehman Brothers. With the worldwide economic crisis now in full swing, and some of the most established investment firms on the planet closing their doors for good, it was obvious Blackstone Group was in deep trouble.

The one silver lining for Blackstone is that they were no rookie to the hospitality game. For the past 15 years, Blackstone had been the world's top investor in the hotel and resort sector, with over 100,000 hotel rooms under their umbrella across the U.S. and Europe. They had extensive experience running successful chains such as La Quinta and Super 8, as well as providing property management for groups like Luxury Resorts. But would that be enough to get them through one of the worst financial crises in history?

The first thing Blackstone focused on at Hilton wasn't real estate values, room rates, marketing campaigns, or anything traditionally associated with profitability. Instead, Blackstone went to work on the corporate culture. Their prior knowledge of the hotel industry meant they knew how to keep employees inspired and provide them with a sense of meaning and purpose. Many investors scoffed at Blackstone for pouring so much money into such intangible aspects of the business, wondering if the firm was losing its edge.

Slowly, Blackstone's work started to pay off. Morale improved. Employees started to feel inspired and grateful about coming to work every day. Most importantly, guests were noticing the difference. Customer satisfaction was climbing fast. But the hotel chain was still hemorrhaging money. If Blackstone didn't stop the bleeding, it wouldn't matter whether Hilton had the happiest employees on the planet. It was time to fix the books.

It turns out the same financial crash that wiped out so much of Hilton's value also presented Blackstone with an opportunity. With interest rates at record lows in the wake of the global market meltdown, the savvy investment firm was able to restructure Hilton's debt in 2010 and save the company billions in unnecessary fees. Soon the hotel was running at a profit again for the first time in years.

By the time Hilton Hotels went public again in 2013, Blackstone had increased the company's value by over $10 billion. They had improved the business astronomically despite horrible market conditions—and they profited handsomely in the process. After the IPO, these bold investors liquidated the majority of their holdings and pocketed a cool $12 billion, earning themselves a place in history. A few years later, in 2018, Blackstone released their remaining 5.79 percent of the company. The sale of those 15.8 million shares generated another $1.45 billion, bringing the full windfall for Blackstone up to nearly $14 billion in profits.

Not a bad upside for a single deal.

Private equity investments are known for having some of the best upside of any asset class. But it's also a highly risky and capital-intensive strategy. Remember, Blackstone had to come up with $27 billion in order to purchase Hilton in a process known as a "leveraged buyout." That's a lot of cash. Most investors don't have that kind of money lying around.

The success of this deal was also largely due to Blackstone's savvy advisors and deep knowledge of the hospitality industry. Many companies went bankrupt during the financial collapse. Hilton could have easily gone out of business and Blackstone could have lost their entire $27 billion. The deal required an extreme level of confidence.

Private equity investing is a way of buying shares in early-stage companies that are not publicly traded on the stock market. Usually, these are smaller companies that need some extra capital in order to grow larger or avoid going broke. Because they are desperate for money, companies like this will often sell a portion of their corporate equity to investors in exchange for capital. If the company goes out of business, the investors lose their money. But if the company gets bought out or goes public at some point, everyone who invested stands to make a lot of money.

Private equity isn't new. This practice has been around since well before the Industrial Revolution and has featured some of the biggest upsides in history. Famously, a group of U.S. business tycoons in the 1800s realized they could make a killing by financing the construction of the Transcontinental Railroad. One such venture, called Central Pacific Railroad, was formed in 1861 by a group of four California businessmen: Collis P. Huntington, Leland Stanford, Mark Hopkins, and Charles Crocker. The fortunes amassed by these individuals as a result of this deal were so large that the men became known as the "Big 4 Railroad Barons". Stanford would ultimately leave his money to open a university outside of San Francisco.

However, it wasn't until after World War II when entrepreneurs established the first true venture capital firms—American Research & Development Corporation and J.H. Whitney & Company—that the private equity business really started booming. In the 1970s, the rise of technology created new opportunities for private equity investors. Venture capital started flowing into small tech companies located in garages, with names like "Apple," "IBM," and "Intel." The returns generated for private equity investors by these companies are still legendary and opened the floodgates for more capital to flow into the venture capital market. Today, most private equity investing is done through investment firms, not by individual investors. The firms raise money from institutional, accredited, and non-accredited investors in order to purchase stakes in private companies.

The most popular types of private equity funding include vulture investing, angel investing (venture capital), leveraged buyouts (LBOs), real estate investment trusts (REITs), and fund of funds (FOF). Some of these I will cover briefly now, while others deserve their own chapters later in the book.

Venture capital investments are generally targeted at small, high-risk start-ups. These start-ups aren't publicly traded and often need investor seed money to grow and potentially go public. Most of the time, venture capitalists aim to ultimately cash out by pushing their companies toward an initial public offering (IPO), merger, or acquisition. At the same time, some companies offer periodic payments to investors, which could incentivize shareholders to let the company continue to grow privately. This is how private equity investments can generate passive income.

In addition to start-up (seed) capital, private equity funds are often used to provide growth capital for mature companies to fund expansions and acquisitions. Well-established companies often require additional infusions of funding in order to open a new branch, develop a new product, attempt a new strategy, or overtake a new competitor. In these cases, both public and private companies may look to private investors to help them get the job done.

Leveraged buyouts are essentially the opposite of IPOs. Instead of taking a company from private to public, LBOs are a way to take public companies and make them private. The goal here is generally for the new private owners to run the company away from the public eye for a few years while looking for ways to make improvements and increase profitability. Then the investors will generally sell the company back to the public on the stock exchange, hoping to turn a profit in the process. LBOs can sometimes be positive for the company—as in the case of Blackstone and Hilton Hotels. Other times, the company can suffer under its new private ownership. It is often possible to increase profits by selling off assets, slashing branches, and terminating employee contracts. Private investors can dismantle a company and then sell it back, functionless, but at a personal profit. Many firms were accused of this practice in the aftermath of the 2008 financial crisis.

Private offerings are typically conducted pursuant to Rule 506(c) of Regulation D, which means private equity firms can solicit investors, but such investors must be government-accredited. This means you'll need to pass a background check and prove that you have a certain amount of capital available to invest. Most accredited investors are high-net-worth individuals or family offices.

Some of the major-player private equity firms are Blackstone, KKR (Kohlberg Kravis Roberts), Carlyle Group, TPG (Texas Pacific Group), and Apollo Global Management. Together, these companies have an astounding $1.3 trillion in assets. In general, firms will keep 20% of any profits from the sale of companies, while their management fees cost 2% annually (an arrangement known as the "2-and-20 structure"). There's a lot of money at stake, so private equity firms generally aren't looking to take risks with non-accredited investors, even when the option to do so does exist legally. Most of the time, private equity firms are looking for accredited investors or institutional investors like pension funds, endowments, banks, or insurance companies.

However, it's possible for anyone to earn passive income from private equity investments, regardless of whether you're accredited or not...

Making Your First Private Equity Investment

Investing in private businesses can be a lot like backpacking without a map. If you know how to navigate, you'll arrive at a beautiful vista, but sometimes even a trail that seems right can have you going in circles for days. Private companies don't have to disclose their business practices or balance sheets in the same way public companies do. Even seasoned investors, who take an active role in each company they own, can be bamboozled by dishonest CEOs.

If you don't want to get lost in the woods, you'll need to understand how private equity investments work.

In the 21st century, it's easier than ever to open and operate a business. Start-ups are sprouting up like weeds. The investment community always seems to be buzzing about the next revolutionary app, groundbreaking biotech product, sustainable technology, or social media darling. Many of these companies set up securities offerings pursuant to Rule 506(b), which allows up to 35 non-accredited investors. Even though 90% of start-ups fail, the chance to invest with a small company is becoming ever more popular. Even non-accredited "layman" investors now have many opportunities to put money into private equity.

If you're looking for this type of opportunity, there are a few different ways you can go.

The first is called direct investing, and it's exactly what it sounds like. You simply approach one or more companies and ask to invest anything from a few thousand dollars to enough to purchase the entire company. The benefit of this approach is that you don't have to pay management fees like you would at a private equity fund. Also, you can get larger returns on your investment because your money won't be spread around like it would be with a fund. However, the risk is also higher. You could lose your money or simply never have the opportunity to "cash out."

Another route for investing in this sector is a private equity fund. This is the most popular and least risky way to get involved. A private equity firm will build a fund and solicit investments from wealthy individuals and institutional investors. Next, the fund management team will use the capital to make investments in a variety of private companies. Everyone who owns shares in the fund will receive profit distributions on an annual or semi-annual basis. Also, fund investors will be paid whenever the firm is able to sell their shares in a company for a profit. The major benefit here is that you gain the experience of an entire team of analysts to manage your investments. That leaves you free to focus on your next deal. Also, this strategy is truly passive, whereas direct investing requires constant work in order to find, buy, manage, and sell equity stakes.

Another option is co-funding, which is essentially a combination of direct and fund investing. If you go this route, a portion of your investment will go to a fund managed by a private equity firm, while another part of your investment will go directly into a company. This is more costly upfront, but it allows you to pay less in management fees and realize a greater potential upside, which can ultimately net you a more impressive return on your capital.

Finally, it is also possible to invest in "secondaries." With this strategy, you might agree to help finance a small company with, say, $5 million. However, you don't have to pay it all at once. You might, for instance, pledge $1 million per year for five years. Unlike pure equity stakes, which cannot be resold to other investors by law, secondaries can be traded on the open market, much like stocks and bonds. If you decide to cash out of your 5-year secondary investment after just 2 years, you can sell either your entire commitment (including the $2 million you already invested) or you can sell parts of your secondary (for instance, you could sell the remaining $3 million commitment) to other limited partners. Secondaries are attractive because they provide a much higher level of liquidity than typical private equity investments.

The biggest concern with private equity is that it's risky and most of the time you'll lose all or most of your money. For skilled investors, the high upside potential more than makes up for this risk. But if you don't know an industry well, it's generally not a good idea to make direct private equity investments. You need to lead the company to success—like Blackstone did for Hilton Hotels—and it's a full-time job that requires a lot of skill. With millions wrapped up in a venture, you'd be a fool to take your eye off the company for even a second, and that can be a lot of work.

If you want that, great. But this is a book on passive income. And the only way to earn truly passive income in the private equity market is to partner with a firm that will manage your investments for you. By selecting a firm with a strong history of success, you'll maximize your profits and minimize your time commitment. You'll have to pay a management fee, but if the team is strong the returns will more than make up for the cost.

Investing in private equity/debt funds with underlying real estate, agriculture, or other tangible income-producing assets can be hugely rewarding and is largely immune to Wall Street volatility. While private equity valuations tend to directionally track the public markets over time, the value of these investments is not subject to the excessive volatility frequently experienced in the public equity markets.

With new firms popping up every year there are now more opportunities than ever to invest in a private equity fund without being an accredited investor. Most firms (maybe 90%) do not partner with unaccredited investors. But the opportunities are still out there. Nascent industries are brimming with young companies hungry for capital and are often willing to offer securities to nonaccredited investors. If you think investing in private companies is for you, here are some tips to help you find the right deal.

When it comes to venture capital investments, you want to look for firms that emphasize revenue growth and are in rapidly growing industries. Such industries could be social media, computer software, or biotechnology. Naturally, growth means more money whether you sell the company or not, and casting your net in booming industries gives you a better chance at catching the next Uber.

While most private equity investors hope to cash out through an IPO, acquisition, or merger, there are many companies that offer periodic income distributions. Once a company you've invested in reaches a critical mass where it can sustain itself and grow steadily, there might be value keeping it in the private sector and continuing to collect regular profits. You could hold a portfolio of these types of private equity stakes that pay out monthly or quarterly checks. Plus, with private equity, your investments are often backed with tangible resources such as real estate, agriculture, or business assets. Even if the company goes south you can still sell off holdings and recoup some or all of your investment. As a limited partner, you are liable in case of a bankruptcy, so it helps to have tangible assets.

It might be advantageous to lower your overall risk by spreading your private equity investments between venture capital, leveraged buyouts, and growth capital simultaneously. While start-ups have a high propensity for failure, well-established companies are generally a safer bet and can allow for a quicker turnaround by using a buy-and-sell approach. For example, it took Facebook eight years to eventually reach a point where it could offer an IPO, whereas restructuring and improving existing companies to improve their value can take as little as two years.

In one case, the Canada Pension Plan Investment Board (CPPIB)—along with private equity firms Silver Lake and Andreessen Horowitz—made an investment in a company called Skype in 2009, purchasing the company from eBay. In 2011, Skype was sold to Microsoft, yielding a $933 million profit to the CPPIB. In two short years, CPPIB more than quadrupled their $300 million investment. Not too shabby.

Private equity investments have enormous upsides. The best way to invest passively is to find a firm that knows what they're doing. This way you can be confident that your companies will grow. Even in the case of failure, which is to be expected in private equity, tangible assets like real estate can protect you from losing all your capital. Long term investments in private companies offering periodic payments, while short-term investments in leveraged buyouts—with the intention of selling companies back to the market—can be extremely profitable and won't command all of your resources.

Next, I'll show you how to use private equity as part of your own passive income machine.

Before You Invest In Private Equity

It's alarming how easily $100 million can disappear. Have you heard of Airware, the revolutionary drone analytics provider? This company had great potential to save contractors a ton of dough by providing bird's eye analytics. With their help, a foreman would no longer have to conduct inspections on site...or send inspectors up to the partially-fabricated 30th floor on a sketchy rig...or rent expensive helicopters to investigate whether or not a certain bolt had been properly installed on a structure 500 feet high.

So why did Airware's investors lose a total of $118 million in the span of a few short years? Because the company couldn't keep up with the competing Chinese drone market. Start-ups fail for endless reasons every single day.

When I first wrote this chapter, Airware had only just failed, but failures are so common in the private equity sphere that Airware's story is old news. A few months earlier, Beepi, an online used-car marketplace, also failed. Juicero, a luxury juicing machine, had the same fate not long after.

In the case of both Beepi and Juicero, $100 million from investors drove right off the lot...or was squeezed into pulp, if you will. But perhaps more shocking than $100 million disappearing twice, is that each of these losses were entirely predictable. Private equity investing, either in startups or venture capital, is highly speculative and leads to failure nine times out of ten. If you want to be an angel investor, you need to be prepared for the likely probability that your equity will vanish entirely, never to be seen again. One way you can protect yourself is to look for a company that offers income distributions to recoup some of your initial investment. You also want to keep an eye out for tangible assets like real estate. This way even when one of your companies loses money you can sell off land, buildings, machinery, or intellectual property to lift some of the bankruptcy burden off the shareholders.

Perhaps the most effective way to invest in the risky private equity market is to hedge your bets by spreading them out. This way you can better stomach the foreseeable losses. It might be worth it to swing and miss on a dozen Beepi's if it means you also knock one out of the park with an investment in Facebook or Airbnb. Or maybe, instead of investing in small companies, you can hunt for a unicorn—a top private company valued at over $1 billion.

Theranos was one of Silicon Valley's unicorns, valued at around $9 billion. It was founded by Stanford researcher Elizabeth Holmes, who became the world's youngest female self-made billionaire through her infamous blood-testing technology. Holmes told investors she had a proprietary procedure that was nothing short of a healthcare revolution. Efficient and life-saving, Theranos tests would supposedly be able to detect a variety of medical conditions from cancer to high cholesterol using just a drop of blood from a painless pin-prick to the finger.

Holmes was bringing in millions of dollars in investor capital, but she refused to reveal how Theranos' technology worked. Holmes demanded signed non-disclosure agreements and hired a security team to escort visitors everywhere—even to the bathroom. This level of secrecy is perfectly legal for a private company, but it leaves investors in the dark.

The problem with the private equity market is that most private companies are essentially a black box. You put your money in and you might get high returns, or you might lose it all, but you don't get to peer inside the box and see how the gears turn.

In August of 2015, the FDA launched a formal investigation into Theranos and revealed "major inaccuracies" with their proprietary testing. Holmes' entrepreneurial success story turned into one of fraud, imprisonment, and crippling fines. By September of 2018, Theranos announced to its shareholders it was shutting down for good, and because the company had few tangible assets investors lost everything. Investing in established private companies can be just as dicey as investing in unproven start-ups.

One way to mitigate the risk of investing in these private start-ups and "unicorns" is to look for transparency. This way you and any investment partners can perform routine checks to ensure the company is on track. However, then this investing strategy may become more time-consuming and stressful than first anticipated.

But even well-researched, legitimate, "safe-bet" buyouts can be catastrophic failures. The mid-2000s were a golden age for these "safe" major buyouts. Perhaps the most famous was the $48 billion acquisition of TXU in 2007 led by KKR, Texas Pacific Group, and Goldman Sachs. It was a bold LBO, but experts were assured that it was the deal of the decade. Even Warren Buffett, famous for his meticulous and savant investment tactics, contributed $900 million.

Investors were keen on the trend that energy prices were skyrocketing. The electricity supply could not keep up with the demand for energy, so it was simple to predict future increased profits for the top energy companies. However, just as soon as the ink had dried on the documents to create Energy Future Holdings, new processes to increase crude oil production were approved for use and the U.S. began a massive push to expand shale oil mining, also known as fracking. The shale gas revolution meant energy prices tumbled, and in 2014 Energy Future Holdings cemented itself as one of the biggest bankruptcies in history.

Even the top private equity investments with the most experienced investors cannot guarantee rich returns. Of course, you might not get the chance to invest in private equity at all if you're not an accredited investor, but there are private investments that are monumentally less risky and more accessible to the average investor, particularly with real estate funds as we will see in the next chapter.

Report Card: Private Equity

Time Commitment: Moderate

Your time commitment can vary greatly depending on your approach to private equity investing. On one hand, you could be a direct investor who is heavily involved with the daily workings of the companies you have stakes in. On the other hand, you could partner with a firm and invest in a managed equity fund. In exchange for management fees, a firm will do the research for you and handle the daily work of keeping the companies on track. Finding the right firm will always take time, but if you want a truly passive approach, paying management fees saves you hundreds of hours each year.

Dealflow: High

There is no shortage of private companies looking for investors. Likewise, private equity firms are constantly looking for new partners. If you're an accredited investor, the opportunities are virtually endless. For non-accredited investors, strong private equity deals are harder to find, but they are definitely out there if you look hard enough.

Capital Commitment: High

Private companies are not looking for a few hundred dollars—or even a few thousand dollars. Running a business is expensive and being able to turn a profit takes a lot of stimulus money, especially in competitive industries. To make a difference in the future of a company, it'll probably cost close to a million (if not many millions) of dollars. On the low end, investment firms usually ask for a minimum of $250,000 to $1,000,000.

Knowledge Requirement: Moderate

Similar to time commitment, your knowledge commitment varies widely based on your approach. If you use a firm to provide the knowledge base, experience, and personnel to lead your company to success, it will require much less study on your end. Conversely, if you decide to make direct investments be prepared to learn exactly what you're doing. It can take years to understand enough about an industry to be successful in the private equity sector.

Return Potential (ROI): Low

There's a fair chance you'll get no return at all investing in private companies. Well-established companies lacking growth potential will often offer periodic profit distributions to stakeholders, but high-growth startups will not. And those are your best bets for the biggest returns. Thus, ROI is pretty low unless you specifically prioritize companies with regular payouts rather than growth potential. Even with regular payments, there's a chance your companies could go under before you get a full return of your capital.

Risk Level: High

You've probably connected the dots: private equity is risky. Some of the best deals might be available only for select individuals and most start-ups inevitably fail. Plus, titanic companies and unicorn companies, as we've seen, can be colossal failures. It's hard to predict which companies will become household names, but it's safe to assume most will never be heard of.

Upside: Ultra-High

When private equity pays off, the upsides are enormous and life-changing. When I talk to other investors, their number one regret is always something along the lines of, "I wish I had invested in Starbucks," or, "I had a chance to invest in Facebook and I passed on it." Silicon Valley is brimming with genius investors who still can't get over their missed opportunity to buy shares in Apple.

The Bottom Line

If you like to gamble, private equity is like an enabling friend. It keeps telling you that the next one will be the "big one." However, failing many times does not mean you are more likely to find success the next time. Playing the numbers game is hard when the minimum investments are so high, but partnering with a reliable firm in a growing industry can boost your odds of striking gold.

Maybe you can tolerate risk and have plenty of capital to play with, and if so, private equity might be for you. But for those who don't want the risk or don't have a million dollars, real estate investing might be a better match. I'll show you what I mean in the next chapter...

Video Assignment #5: Problems in the Stock Market

By now you know that private equity is incredibly risky, but the payoff can be astronomical if you choose the right investments. In this chapter's video, let's zoom out and look at the stock market in general.

The stock market only increases 3.9% per year after inflation and demonstrates a high level of volatility. To build generational wealth, it is best to only keep a small portion of your assets in common stock, if any.

To access the video, go to passiveincomethebook.com/5.

CHAPTER 6

Active Real Estate Investing

Long before he ever bought his first building or made his first million dollars, Sam Zell was a teenage boy obsessed with a new magazine called *Playboy*. Released in 1953, the first issue sold 70,000 copies within days of hitting shelves. Word of the tantalizing magazine spread like wildfire: businessmen, factory workers, college students, and schoolboys alike all scrambled to get their hands on a copy. Perhaps nobody, however, drooled harder at the sight of that first *Playboy* issue than Sam Zell. Except, Sam wasn't interested for the reasons you might think...

Sam was born to Polish refugees, Ruchla and Berek Zielonka, who moved to Chicago, Illinois (the Polish capital of America) in 1941. Wanting a proper Jewish education for their son, the couple enrolled Sam at the best Hebrew school they could find, in the suburbs. As a teen Sam noticed during his daily commute from the city that Playboy magazine was well-supplied downtown, but was not available outside the city limits.

Sensing an entrepreneurial opportunity, Sam purchased as many of the modern magazines as he could carry from a downtown newsstand for $0.50 a pop. In the afternoon he resold the *Playboy* magazines to his classmates at a whopping $3 each—a 500% mark-up. The profit potential of these magazines excited Sam much more than the jaw-dropping centerfolds. He realized buying low and selling high could make him rich. By the time he was in college, Sam was beginning to apply the same method to real estate.

Ever since the day he risked all of his meager allowance on reselling *Playboy* magazines, Sam started to equate risk with reward. So when a local landlord purchased a distressed apartment building, Sam saw an opportunity and convinced the man to hire him as a property manager. Not many people are willing to take risks, such as buying an apartment complex with rusty gutters, broken windows, flaking paint, and cracked siding. But Sam was attracted to risk.

All of those afternoons on the playground selling magazines had endowed Sam with the instincts of a salesman. He tactfully persuaded his fellow students at the University of Michigan to move in. With Sam in charge it didn't take long for the complex to fill completely. In just a few months, the formerly rundown building was turning a hefty profit.

Sam had demonstrated not just to the landlord, but to himself, that he could turn a failing property into a major success. The profit margins were much bigger than his magazine redistribution scheme and he was hungry from more ventures into real estate.

In school, Sam was studying to become a lawyer, but outside of his studies he expanded his role as a property manager. By the time law school graduation rolled around Sam was successfully managing about 5,000 apartments in Ann Arbor, Michigan.

Despite not being thrilled about a career as a lawyer, Sam took a job as an attorney anyway. As he predicted, he hated it. He spent hours behind a desk every day and found the work boring. Sam wanted to do what he was good at: managing properties. But managing properties wasn't exactly "passive." It wasn't something he could do on the side while working full time.

After a year with the law firm, Sam called it quits and used his property management knowledge to form Equity Properties Management Corporation with a partner. The real estate firm handled scouting, acquisition, and management while Sam quickly evolved his skills from that of a property manager to those of a top-tier salesman. Soon, he brought in massive investments from friends, colleagues, and acquaintances all eager to get in on the action. Over the next few years, Sam raised millions from investors and used the capital to purchase a diverse range of properties. Eventually, he came to control thousands of rental properties and was incredibly wealthy.

Today, Sam is eighty years old. He doesn't have to lift a finger to manage his properties; he has a whole team in place to scout new buildings and find tenants for him. In other words, Sam is no longer an active real estate investor. These days, his income is entirely passive.

Many of the world's top real estate moguls followed this exact same progression. They started their career investing actively in rental properties and eventually shifted to a more passive role.

The story is the same for me, minus the **Playboy** resale venture. When I started in real estate investing I did everything myself. And I made a lot of mistakes. I lost money on some properties and made money on others. But most importantly, I learned what worked. That experience allowed me to hire a team, one person at a time, and train them to handle everything. These days my team makes a profit on virtually every deal—and we collect passive income for years on each property we buy.

Active real estate investing is a lot of work. It quickly becomes a full-time job once you own a few hundred rental units. But if you have the time and interest to get into this field, it is a phenomenal way to build long-term passive income. Developing an acumen for real estate can take years, but the massive returns can outweigh the slow start.

Everyone knows it "takes money to make money." The phrase is so overused it's become an entrepreneurial platitude. What fewer people understand—and what most real estate managers will hide when asking for your investment dollars—is that 95% of people trying to break into real estate fail. Your best bet at success is either to study the masters, research market conditions, and put in a ton of active work...*or*, outsource your education and heavy lifting to a team with a lot of experience. Both of these options have pros and cons. In this chapter, I'll focus on active investing, and in the next chapter, I'll get into passive real estate strategies.

It's completely possible that after buying a property and hiring managers, contractors, and listing agents, you might walk away with a net profit of about $100-$200 per month. That is a LOT of work for a hundred bucks. Why would anyone get into real estate with that kind of return? The answer is simple: it is scalable. With each property you invest in, the work gets easier. You start to learn trends, you improve your analytical skills, and you grow your network. While the first property deal might take months to close, the second, third, and fourth ones will be right around the corner.

You'll be surprised at how quickly you can arrive at a hundred properties. Even at a profit margin of just $100 each this nets you $10,000 in passive income each month. As I explained earlier, I was able to go from zero properties to over 100 in less than five years. That's when I quit my job and became a full-time real estate investor.

When you invest actively in real estate, the goal is always to eventually bring on employees who can take over the jobs you don't want to do. Eventually, you can replace your current salary with rental income and quit your job, like I did. Then you can devote more time to finding the kind of real estate deals that will make you truly rich. That's one of the fastest ways in the world to achieve complete financial independence. But it's also more work than any of the other approaches I will cover in this book—a lot more work. Active real estate investing will take over your life for years until you can build a team to handle the management for you.

If that appeals to you, this asset class might be your ticket. On the other hand, if you're interested in the amazing investment potential of real estate but don't have the time to devote 50+ hours a week to scouting, purchasing, and managing properties, you're a great candidate for passive real estate investing, which I'll cover shortly.

For now, let's focus on how you can get your first property, learn as much as is necessary in order to be successful, and exponentially grow your portfolio until you can replace your day job with monthly checks from real estate ventures.

What It Takes to Make It in Real Estate

Most new real estate investors fail because they started before they were ready. They dove in too soon without being properly prepared. Don't become a statistic. Perform these three checks to judge if the timing is right for you.

1: Are You Ready Financially?

If you don't have enough capital to get started in real estate on your own, don't borrow the cash from someone else. That's a recipe for disaster. Wait until you have enough money saved up to cover the startup costs yourself, plus an extra 10-20%, because something will inevitably go wrong. Typically, you'll want to have enough funding to cover a 20-25% down payment on the value of the property in order to secure a real estate loan or mortgage. You'll also need additional capital to cover any repairs or construction. We'll call that the "rehab cost." And there are two other less obvious, but completely necessary, expenses to budget for: holding and closing costs.

Holding costs are operational expenses. This number refers to how much cash you need to spend on a monthly or yearly basis to keep the property functioning, including taxes, cleaning services, insurance, and mortgage payments. Every house will have a different holding cost, so you'll need to accurately appraise the operational burden of a property before you buy. As an example, older structures or shoddily built new ones may require greater holding costs.

Closing costs are also highly variable. The closing cost is how much you'll have to spend (or subtract from your profits) after you sell a property. This generally encompasses all sorts of fees: fees to straighten out the title, fees for the attorney handling the transaction, fees for the real estate agent, and fees to list and market the property. There's a lot you can do to reduce closing costs, but you'll inevitably have to shell out something even in a "no closing cost" scenario. It's wise to estimate this cost before purchasing a property so you can prepare for the reality that you'll eventually have to sell. If you need to sell down the road to prevent a net loss, you don't want to get surprised by lofty closing costs you didn't factor in.

There are many ways to secure capital to fund a real estate investment, and the best choice is different for everybody. For some it's a high-paying job, like being a lawyer, doctor, or entertainer. For others it's coming into inheritance money, receiving a bonus, or winning a cash prize. For Sam Zell, it was saving up funds from good old-fashioned hard work and a frugal lifestyle. Regardless, in order to invest in real estate, you'll need to have a stable financial record and be able to prove to the bank that you can weather any pop-up storms. On top of liquid assets, you'll need a decently sized emergency fund.

An emergency fund, as discussed in Chapter 3, usually consists of 6-12 months of your typical income stashed away in a highly liquid form in case things go wrong (and they usually do). The importance of an emergency fund speaks to the bottom line when it comes to real estate investment: don't get into real estate because you're struggling, do it because you're comfortable and want more.

The good news is that "comfortable" doesn't mean you need to save up the entire cost of a property in cash before getting started. You can safely take out a loan to fund your rental properties because the tenants will pay off the mortgage for you.

The numbers should work out to where the tenant's rent covers the mortgage and any property management costs with a few hundred dollars leftover for you to pocket. Properties that fully cover the monthly costs and still yield a monthly profit are considered cash-flow positive. With these kinds of properties, as soon as you close escrow and find a tenant you'll start making money. At the same time, you'll be gaining equity in the property each month for free. That's not a bad deal.

However, because rental income is considered 'active,' the taxes can be steep. You'll want to research the best deductions to reduce your tax burden. These are different in every state and can take many hours of research to understand, but they can save you buckets of money. This brings me to the next item on your checklist before you go out looking for your first investment property.

2: Can You Sacrifice Time for Learning?

The fact that you're reading this book means you're already off to a good start, but reading isn't the only tool you'll need in order to beat the odds and become successful as an active real estate investor. The hardest part of the learning curve is finding the time to research all the ins and outs of a potential deal. Let's consider some of the main time-drains you should prepare for before buying a property.

The best way to protect yourself against unknowns is to familiarize yourself with every stage of the deal from opening to closing and to vet a team of mentors who can fill you in on what you missed. There's no way around it: you'll have to set aside some time to learn so you don't become another sucker who thinks they can make it big without any experience. It's an expensive mistake to skip the educational process.

It's possible to pick up real estate jobs and educate yourself through on-the-ground experience, like Sam Zell did when he worked as a property manager in college. Many successful real estate investors have done this, or at least chosen to be hands-on at the beginning of their real estate careers so they could rapidly acquire knowledge. Your first deal is likely going to take months, so you might as well use that time to study. The more you know, the faster you can buy new properties with the confidence of an expert.

In the real estate world, house-flipping is not easy or cheap, and it's almost guaranteed to cost you more than it will make you. It might make great reality TV, but flipping is not a sound business model unless you can buy in cash and stay current on the ins-and-outs of the changing laws and market trends. What works in the real estate world is long-term investing that is well-researched. It's not sexy, but it's proven.

3: Do You Want to Become Your Own Boss?

If you have the time to learn the ropes, nor the assets to back up your investments, the last question to ask yourself is whether you are ready to become your own boss. Active real estate investing is perfect for the investor who wants to start their own property management company and hire people to work for them. But before you get to that point, you'll have to do it all yourself first.

When you start out in real estate everything is on you. It can be incredibly rewarding when things go well, but it's also a big lifestyle adjustment. If you're not ready for the unstructured schedule that comes with leaving your job to pursue entrepreneurial ventures full time, you might not maximize your potential. This is why I'd suggest getting started in real estate on the side while keeping your steady job for as long as possible.

One benefit of this approach is that you can experience property management in a low-risk environment and decide whether the active real estate lifestyle is for you before you make a dramatic leap of faith. It's also a huge help to have a source of income to rely on while you're taking risks and paying the 'tax' of learning the ropes. It's reasonable to assume that off the bat you might experience losses, a longer return on investment, or unexpected vacancies that could threaten the sustainability of your new money-making vehicle. Plus, you won't be making sizable passive income right away, so you can use the paychecks from your day job to finance property managers and other real estate professionals to help get your first investment off the ground.

It can be scary, but once you have a few properties under your belt and a few monthly checks rolling in, becoming your own boss starts to sound a lot more pleasant.

That covers the top three factors you need to assess before you get into active real estate investing. It's a huge commitment in both capital and time to get started, and being able to venture into the unknown takes great strength of will! However, if you can handle the ups and downs as well as the inevitability of dealing with and managing people, this might be the investment strategy for you. In the next section, I'll tell you some tricks of the trade I've developed to help you find the right property on your first buy.

How I Find My Real Estate Investments

Buying a house is one of the biggest financial decisions most people make in their entire life. For most of us, choosing a home is not just about dollars and cents, but where we want to spend the rest of our lives. Homes are meaningful. This is why even short-term renters don't take choices lightly. Many agonize over the decision of where to live for months before finally pulling the trigger.

For real estate investors, this means it might not always be easy to find tenants who will agree to rent your properties. And for every month your real estate sits vacant you'll still be subject to holding costs, not to mention mortgage payments. The quality of the neighborhood is one major litmus test many buyers look at to determine the potential of an investment property. When you're searching for the right rental, it's a good idea to locate a neighborhood with a recent history of appreciating values. In other words, you want to find an area that is up and coming so your investment becomes more valuable over time.

The Bay Area, California, is an extreme, albeit informative, case study because investors and homeowners in the region have accumulated so much net worth through property that it's now considered a 'crisis' market and most outsiders and low-income residents cannot afford to live there anymore. One element that can help you predict a booming real estate market is the economic opportunities in a given region. In the case of San Francisco, it was the flourishing of the tech industry in Silicon Valley that ultimately drove housing prices through the roof. Buying real estate before the tech boom would have made you rich. But now most investors would be crazy to get started there because prices are so high. It's hard to imagine the economy in San Francisco exploding like that again any time soon.

Another test many investors swear by is to purchase properties near high-end retailers such as Whole Foods, Apple, or Lululemon. If these savvy companies have recently invested in a particular neighborhood, there's a good chance the area is poised to spike in value. Some investors track future locations of Starbucks to predict up-and-coming neighborhoods and markets. But a competitive, burgeoning region isn't the only predictor of rapid appreciation.

The next factor to investigate is simply supply and demand. Career real estate investors are always scouting neighborhoods that can't expand due to geographic or legislative constraints. A common strategy is looking at college and university neighborhoods. In that respect, Sam Zell was ahead of the game. A market with an endless supply of land will never appreciate to the same degree as the limited surface area of San Francisco, New York City, or a sandy beach front. As the saying goes, you can't make more Hawai'i.

It is often effective to wait for a neighborhood to 'fall out of style' or face a heightened rate of foreclosures, as many communities experienced following the housing crisis. This strategy ensures more bang for your buck because when prices go back up, you'll reap upsides. However, pay attention to vacancies when investing in a distressed or high demand neighborhood so you don't get duped.

A neighborhood with a high vacancy rate can eviscerate your portfolio because when buildings are vacant, you're missing one of the most important pieces of the real estate puzzle: tenants. Tenants are what make active real estate investing possible. They cover your mortgage, pay your rent, and allow you to expand your empire. It can take dozens of tenants before you'll be able to turn a serious profit on your real estate holdings. But even one property standing vacant can cost you thousands per month in holding costs. Vacancies are the mortal enemy of the real estate investor.

Discovering the right property at the right price can take years of real estate acumen, especially if you aren't closely tuned-in to the markets where you're investing. It can be discouraging to go through all the work of purchasing a property and finding a tenant only to realize you still need to find 99 more before your enterprise will be making real money. Good deals won't just show up on your doorstep, you have to hunt for them. Like any skill, though, it gets easier with practice. The more you learn, the faster and simpler the next deal becomes. The trick is not to buy linearly (e.g., 2 properties every year), but, rather, to buy exponentially (e.g., double your properties every year). This is how you can get to 100 properties in just a few short years.

It might take you 6 months to close your first deal, but with the local knowledge and network you gain, you should be able to buy your next two properties in another 6-month timeframe. At the end of a year, let's say you have three properties. Go for three more in the next 6 months. Double it again, and you're at 12 properties in 2 years. You can see where this is going...

Active real estate investing is not easy, but it is worth it for those who stick it out. If you work hard and analyze your markets carefully, you can become a real estate big shot. It doesn't matter if you're a first-generation American whose parents don't speak English, like Sam Zell, a top celebrity like Ellen DeGeneres (who's netted $150 million in real estate deals), or a music agent at William Morris. You just need to be ready to roll up your sleeves and put in the work.

Report Card: Active Real Estate Investing

Time Commitment: High

Active real estate investing can be one of the most time-draining investment options because it requires so much research and knowledge to get started. Plus, these deals aren't open and shut; there are a lot of hoops to jump through, which can be overwhelming to a newcomer. To accomplish future goals, you'll probably end up hiring a team to do the leg work for you, which can save you thousands of hours of work. But in the beginning, you're going to be handling most everything by yourself.

Dealflow: Average

Sometimes you'll hear the terms "buyer's market" and "seller's market" thrown around. This is because real estate can fluctuate wildly depending on the specific area and on the global economy. In general, there are always plenty of properties available. However, there may not be many options that make sense as investment properties. These deals are rarer and often require months of sleuthing to uncover.

Capital Commitment: High

A down payment might seem like a hefty price to pay, but it isn't impossible. For a $200,000 single-family home, you might pay as little as $10,000 down if you have great credit. However, rehab costs can easily surpass most down payments. Active real estate investing can have you hemorrhaging dollars if you don't do your research. Plus, you'll need more than a couple properties if you want enough passive income to positively affect your lifestyle. As a long-term strategy, a lot of capital is required.

Knowledge Requirement: High

Most real estate investors fail before their sophomore year because they make poor investment choices and are overwhelmed by what they don't know. You can rise above the rest with a professional knowledge base. To master active real estate investing you need to hit the books, or at least hire experts with the knowledge necessary for success. There is much to learn.

Return Potential (ROI): High

Real estate offers great long-term return potential because it is scalable. You could get lucky and earn a return of $500 per month off of a killer property, but it's more likely that you'll earn between $100-$200. What's beautiful is that a lot of properties are immediately cash flow positive, so while the ROI on a single property isn't anything to write home about, scaling your business can lead to cumulative returns that will put you in the 1%.

Risk Level: High

There's no end to the dangers that can put your property at risk. Vacancies, damage, unexpected rehab costs, declining market conditions, you name it. These setbacks are not cheap and can easily dismantle your portfolio if you're not careful. It's high risk, high reward.

Upside: Moderate

Property appreciation is what attracts most people to active real estate investing. Buying a $250,000 property that becomes a $500,000 property in ten years is realistic in the right area. But it isn't common. Historically, real estate appreciates at about 3% per year—just enough to keep pace with inflation. The real key to making money in real estate is to purchase properties that are immediately cash flow positive.

The Bottom Line

Real estate is a risky, costly, and highly competitive industry. It's not for everyone, which is why there's such a huge payoff for those who stick with it. Once you reach 100 properties, you'll likely have also built up the know-how, team, and acumen necessary to take your hands off the wheel. The learning curve is steep, and so is the initial capital to get started, but it's completely worth it if you're committed to weather the first few years. Every property you buy will make the process a little bit easier and a little quicker. Before you know it, you could be buying dozens of properties in the timeframe of a few months.

Active real estate investing will take over your life for years until you can build a team to handle the management for you. If you're interested in the amazing investment potential of real estate but don't have the time to devote 50+ hours a week to scouting, purchasing, and managing properties, you're a great candidate for passive real estate investing, which I'll cover in the next chapter. And I'll show you how Christopher Columbus used this same basic investment structure to fund his mission to the new world...

Video Assignment #6: Hedge Against Inflation

Why is real estate such an enticing investment? It is a hard asset. In this chapter's video, we'll take a look at the general benefit of hard assets. Hard assets can help protect your wealth from inflation across generations. When investing in a hard asset such as real estate, the primary benefit is that you can protect yourself twice because rent can be increased each year and the underlying value of the property will subsequently increase.

To access the video, go to passiveincomethebook.com/6.

CHAPTER 7

Private Real Estate Lending

Actively buying and managing real estate is incredibly lucrative but it's also a lot of work, which is why most people eventually transition from an active role to a passive one.

With passive investing, you'll be the one putting up the money so someone else can go buy properties and rent them out. In exchange, the borrower will agree to pay you a fixed amount every month until your initial investment has been paid back, plus interest. This practice is nothing new. In fact, one of the most famous expeditions of all time was set up using a nearly identical arrangement.

The year was 1484 and a 33-year-old merchant named Christopher Columbus had just been royally rejected by King John II of Portugal. Columbus had hoped to borrow a bit of cash to finance one of the boldest real estate ventures of all time. He proposed to cross the Atlantic and claim millions of acres in untouched land for the Portuguese crown as well as rights to a new water trade route. All Columbus needed from King John II was a loan of two million gold maravedis—around $40 million today.

King John II, however, was not convinced. The mission was too risky; the cost, too high. Plus, Portugal was in a secure spot financially and didn't need to take on the high-risk, high-reward venture. The king dismissed

Columbus, saying he didn't want any part of the merchant's crazy scheme.

Frustrated, but not ready to give up on his dreams, Columbus decided to head to the neighboring country of Spain and try his luck there with the new King Ferdinand and Queen Isabella. Unlike King John, the Spanish monarchs were interested in Columbus' offer. The idea of claiming acres and acres of pristine land—and all of the natural resources contained therein—for the Spanish Crown excited them. However, Ferdinand and Isabella were strapped for cash at the moment. They were forced to pay 24 million maravedis to the Moors to get them to vacate Granada and they simply didn't have an extra two million lying around to offer Columbus.

Disappointed but not deterred, Columbus spent six long years in Spain trying to convince the king and queen to change their minds. He was able to raise a quarter of the money (500 thousand maravedis) from wealthy investors. But he knew he couldn't raise all two million in the private sector because his mission required the blessing of a monarch. Columbus needed an investor who could defend any claims he made on the land and riches he came across during his travels. Only royal investors had that kind of power.

Finally, eight years later, in 1492, Columbus received word from Ferdinand and Isabella that they'd been able to borrow some money from neighboring countries and were ready to invest in his expedition. Their agreement with Columbus stipulated that he would be entitled to a small share of the profits from the voyage, he would earn the prestigious title of "Admiral of the Ocean Sea", and he would be appointed "Viceroy and Governor" of all lands he was able to claim in the name of Spain. In exchange, the Crown was entitled to the lion's share of gold and jewels obtained during the expedition.

And Spain was to own the land Columbus discovered.

When Columbus signed the agreement and set out across the Atlantic, he had no idea he'd just put together one of the most successful real estate finance deals of all time. The investment provided by Ferdinand and Isabella would end up multiplying the size of their kingdom exponentially in just a few months and make Spain the new world power.

Today, there isn't much acreage that would lend itself to a Columbus-style land-grab deal (unless you're into extraterrestrial real estate ventures of the Mars variety). However, the type of arrangement Columbus made with Ferdinand and Isabella is still very much alive.

Secured private real estate lending is a practice where developers or property managers (known as "borrowers") obtain financing for real estate deals directly from private investors (known as "sponsors") rather than going to banks or institutional lenders. This is also known as "hard money" lending.

Sponsoring real estate investments comes with many of the same risks associated with active real estate investing. One major benefit to this type of loan compared to other investments (like private equity) is that your principal will always be at least partially secured by the tangible asset of the property itself—which you can always sell if your borrower isn't able to flip the property or find renters in a reasonable timeframe.

Another benefit to this type of investment is flexibility. As a secured private lender, you can adjust the interest rate however you'd like as well as the payment schedule, equity split, restrictions, and any other aspects of the deal. Because these contracts are essentially agreements between two or more individuals, there are fewer rules, requirements, and regulations to deal with. Queen Isabella, for instance, added a few additional stipulations (like the exclusive ability to sell licenses to traders at port cities in the new world) to her contract with Columbus to sweeten the pot. If you're nervous about lending your riches on a deal that might go south, you can always find creative ways to hike up the benefits on your side of the arrangement and make it worth your while. In general, flexibility is one of the biggest advantages to private lending.

While there are limits to the number of loans you can dole out without a license (based on your local regulations), you generally have plenty of freedom. There are many private lending companies out there that provide a similar service. However, they are typically far stricter about the terms, conditions, and rates of their finance deals than individual private lenders can be. Individuals can also loan out their funds in far less time than a private lending company can, with fewer hoops to jump through, which is a major draw for many investors. This means there is a vast market for individual sponsors to compete with large companies, strike highly advantageous deals with borrowers, and build strong, professional relationships with a large web of individual investors.

As the sponsor, you set the terms for your deals. Your terms can be different for each partner and each property you consider. The interest rates you can expect to receive range anywhere from 4% to upwards of 10%. It's entirely within your rights as a private lender to ask for 15% interest on your loan, with the main caveat being competition from other lenders who might offer a better rate to a potential borrower. Ten percent is a powerful interest rate, especially given that your loan is secured by the underlying value of the property being purchased.

Another huge benefit of being a secured private real estate lender is that the deals come to you. For instance, Columbus spent six years petitioning the king and queen begging them to invest in his venture. They didn't have to come up with the idea themselves or do any of the work to get it off the ground. The opportunity simply fell into their lap. Similarly, once you can establish yourself as a private real estate lender, investors hungry for capital will start lining up around the block for a chance to pitch you their investment idea. This significantly cuts the amount of work you have to do to find quality deals. They literally come to you. And the better your reputation gets—and the more capital you amass—the more Columbus-sized deals will start to present themselves.

Getting started can be one of the toughest things about private real estate lending. After all, if borrowers don't know you exist, they can't seek you out and pitch deals to you. Relationships are paramount for private lenders. You'll need a strong web of relationships within the real estate industry to ensure adequate deal flow. This is why many private lenders start out as active real estate investors. After a few years, they've built up enough capital and made enough connections to finance deals for other investors.

When you're looking for borrowers to make your money work for you through real estate investing, it's never a bad idea to start with friends, family, and business associates. Especially if you know some people who have prior success in real estate.

Another advantage of starting out as an active investor before transitioning to private lending is that prior experience can help you learn what to look for when analyzing a new deal. If you have the capital but lack experience, you can always hire outside help (such as accountants and appraisers) to help you judge the quality of potential loan agreements. Either way, it's much more passive to be a lender than to participate in active real estate investing. The reduced time burden allows you to spend more of your resources analyzing the quality of each deal and running the numbers on title fees and rehab costs than worrying about the long list of steps required to open and close the deal yourself.

In the rest of this chapter, I'll go over what you need to do to prepare yourself to become a private real estate investor, as well as the red flags you should look out for when meeting with potential borrowers. If you have the capital to finance private real estate loans, you don't want to overlook this opportunity. Your money won't be sitting around at a low interest rate, it will accomplish real growth and rehab the real estate assets in your area (or abroad). It will also fill the need for quick financing among developers who have all the parameters figured out—minus the funding.

You can enjoy the prestige of being real estate royalty while financing eager and accomplished borrowers who are ready to discover the next big prospect as soon as they can secure the necessary funds.

Rookie Mistakes In Real Estate Lending

Before you run out and start lending money to every real estate developer you can find, it would be prudent to spend some time studying a few historical real estate deals that turned out to be epic failures. Why not the successes? Feel free to study those, but I'm particularly interested in avoiding major pitfalls and costly blunders. As the saying goes, "Those who cannot remember the past are condemned to repeat it." Learn the mistakes of the past before getting started in any new business endeavor.

Throughout history, many leaders have failed to heed the lessons of their predecessors. When Adolf Hitler invaded Russian soil in the fall of 1941, winter was just around the corner. He was so sure his superior Aryan troops could crush the Russian army and return home before the first snowfall that his soldiers didn't even bring jackets. Apparently, Hitler forgot to read his history books, because Napoleon made a similar blunder during the French Invasion of 1812. Half of Napoleon's nearly 400,000-strong army was wiped out by the freezing cold during the first eight weeks of the conquest. Battered at every campaign on his way to Moscow, Napoleon eventually retreated in what historians now consider a "self-defeat."

Similarly, Napoleon could have avoided this crippling error had he taken the time to learn from the mistakes of the past. Just over one hundred years previously, in 1707, the Swedish army had marched east into Russia under the command of King Charles XII. Instead of putting up a fight at the border, the Russians fell back, burning anything and everything of value that stood between them and the Swedes. Unable to harvest wood for fire, hunt any animals, or construct any type of lasting shelter, King Charles' army largely starved or succumbed to the freezing temperatures.

This is not to say that I wish Hitler, Napoleon, or Charles, had been successful—not at all. I bring up these avoidable failures because I've found the same phenomenon in the real estate world: most new investors waste vast amounts of capital making avoidable mistakes that would be obvious to any seasoned investor. They repeat history instead of taking the time to learn from it.

What follows is my best advice for getting started as a secured private real estate lender. These basic ground rules are based on years of experience and research in this industry and will help you avoid 98% of the major pitfalls. But you can't learn everything about passive real estate investing from a single chapter in a book. If you're truly serious about entering into private equity lending, my best advice is to spend a few months reading and learning about as many previous deals as you can. Study what went wrong.

When I was first starting out in real estate, I connected with over a dozen big investors all across the country. I traveled to their home cities and took each one out to lunch (at the swankiest restaurant in town) to ask about their experiences. Most importantly, I asked about their mistakes. Could they tell me about a deal they lost money on? Why did they lose money? What are they doing differently now as a result of that experience?

By studying the mistakes of the past before I got started, I was able to avoid many of the pitfalls that trap the new or average investor and was able to start out on the right foot. (As an added bonus, these lunches netted me a handful of relationships with top names in the industry, which proved to be just as valuable as the stories I heard.)

One of the big things I learned was that there are a few crucial talking points to raise with a potential borrower before you agree to deliver a loan. First and foremost, it's important to negotiate whether the loan will be assessed based on the property's current value, or post-repair value. There is typically a big difference between the two. You'll want to base your loan on the initial value because repair costs are often vastly underestimated by the borrower. This is one of the most common mistakes made by rookie lenders.

Also, you should find out how much money the investor is willing to bring to the table. If your borrower falls short and doesn't have enough cash for the needed repairs, you don't want to be in a position where you need to invest even more to save the property. Instead, it can be preferable for the borrower to pay out of pocket or find another sponsor to cover unbudgeted rehab costs. These costs are incurred due to the borrower's failure to accurately predict the capital required for repairs. That means it's their fault and the difference should be deducted from their profits on the deal.

When a borrower runs out of money you'll be in for an expensive, time-consuming foreclosure. So I've found it's best to always hire an independent appraiser to give a more accurate (or second opinion) rehab estimate. Another way to dodge this bullet is to include additional fees in your contract with the borrower. For instance, every time your borrower misses a deadline or gets an estimate wrong it adds risk to your loan. To protect yourself, add some fees to increase your returns on a dubious deal. It's important to be clear up front that these fees exist. Don't hide them in the fine print.

You can also safeguard against a bad deal by making a schedule to disburse funds to the borrower, which you can back out of at any time. This is more advantageous compared to providing the entire sum in a single lump payment upfront because if anything goes wrong with the deal you can cancel future payments. Plus, the great thing about real estate investing is that you're secured by the asset of tangible property. It gives you the flexibility to purchase the property outright from a novice borrower so you can finish the job yourself or sell it off before it becomes a money sinkhole.

Long story short, you can't do these deals over dinner and cocktails.

And you shouldn't try to do an entire deal on your own. If you don't already have a team in place, rent one. Hire a lawyer and an accountant to analyze tax implications, assess risk, and create a protocol for reviewing incoming deals. If Napoleon had a better advisor, perhaps the Russian capital would now be named *Moscou* and fur-lined berets would be common winter headware. (The implications of Hitler avoiding failure in Russia, however, does not lend itself to any pleasant thoughts in my mind). When an accountant reaches a verdict on the quality of the deal, they can help you decide on an appropriate interest rate and timeline to ensure you'll be earning fair compensation for the risk you take on.

Generally speaking, you want to aim for around 10% interest to account for risk on a private real estate deal. Additionally, your accountant will likely suggest risking only a fraction of your capital on a single property, as even the most competent borrowers can make mistakes. The following red flags are ten things to watch out for when a new investor approaches you for a private real estate loan.

1. Fast deals spell disaster. Anyone in a hurry might be overlooking crucial details, or plan to aim for a quick flip instead of a quality long term investment.

2. An absence of history presents a blind spot. You want to look for people with a good track record so you can study their successes and shortcomings. First-timers are more likely to fail.

3. Interest rates that are too high can indicate scams. If the deal sounds too good to be true, it probably is. Be wary of investors trying to sell you on interest rates over 20%—there's likely something fishy going on and you're not being shown the whole picture.

4. Poor investors are poor candidates. If your investor is looking for a loan because they're broke, you might be putting your eggs in a holey basket. A get-rich-quick mentality can cause oversight

and too much optimism; if the investor's budget falls short, they will have no capital to continue the project and might ask you for more or you may end up foreclosing.

5. Beware of the DIY guy. Any investor bent on doing the rehab themselves invites a world of potential hurdles. Unless they are a licensed contractor with stellar references, a DIY approach is doomed to become a string of missed deadlines and unreliable craftsmanship. Even if the final project passes inspection, work that is not up to par can cause extra expenses down the road.

6. Large loans can hurt you more than the investor. As a rule of thumb, you want to pool funds with your investor and never lend more than two-thirds of the after-repair value. You don't want to loan too much because a foreclosure will cost you thousands.

7. A bad pitch begets bad execution. The pitch is an opportunity to assess how the prospective investors conduct themselves professionally. If they're missing data, underperform, or raise more questions than answers, that might predict more faults to come. Don't rely on references or personality alone. If they are serious about the deal, they will at least be able to answer all your questions and concerns.

8. A follower might not be a leader. If you're meeting with an investor who bases all of their insight on what other investors are doing, they might be missing the fundamental concepts behind a wise investment: thinking for oneself. Worse yet, they might not know how to step up and face an emergency.

9. Too many projects equal less oversight on each. While there are investors who take too long to complete a single project, others may be overly eager and spread themselves too thin. If your investor is taking on too many projects at once, they'll all come out half-baked.

10. If you can't talk with them, don't work with them. This red flag covers a lot of ground. You don't have to become best friends with every borrower who comes your way, but even a good prospective deal can go bad if you can't communicate effectively. Plus, an investor who is aloof might be playing the field with mass outreach instead of taking you seriously.

Save yourself the hassle of making rookie mistakes. As we've seen, it's possible to avoid getting stranded on a Russian tundra if you take the time to learn from your predecessors. And you don't have to take them each out to lunch to do so. While market conditions are always in flux, some guidelines are eternal when it comes to private real estate loans.

How to Build Your Real Estate Network

Before you run out and start offering loans for real estate development projects, it's a good idea to get some real-world experience in the industry. This is the first step in becoming a real estate titan. Think about it this way: what kind of a patient would hire a surgeon who hasn't completed their medical education? Probably a desperate patient without any other options. Similarly, what kind of borrowers are going to seek a loan from a first-time lender with no experience in the real estate industry? Almost exclusively novices who don't have any experience or credentials themselves.

The best and most reliable borrowers aren't looking to partner with an unschooled lender. Before you put your chips down as a private lender, you will likely need to put in a few years of work actively investing in properties. Practice from managing a few rental properties can help you make smarter decisions around rehab costs and the potential for foreclosure. Trying your hand at property management will also give you direct experience predicting which properties might flourish and which might flounder. This way, you'll have a better feel for numbers and neighborhoods. You'll increase your deal flow as a sponsor and boost the confidence of your borrowers (and yourself). Plus, the risk on your loans will decrease drastically. But prior real estate experience isn't the only factor at play when getting into private lending.

Before you set off on your search for borrowers you'll want to make sure you can afford to loan out your capital—especially when that loan might not mature. A popular funding source for a private real estate loan is your IRA or 401k. However, you should never loan out so much that a fore-closure would jeopardize your ability to retire safely and comfortably. It's important to be prepared to lose it all before making any large investment. Of course, you'll do everything you can to avoid this scenario, but it remains a possibility.

If you're financially equipped to take the risk of becoming a lender, the next readiness test is your network. It's hard to start a new business without clients, so building a contact list is crucial. If you've spent time in the real estate industry, you should have an ample supply of trustworthy investors who might want to partner and borrowers who would be open to borrowing from you. Alternatively, it can be extremely valuable to search outside of the world of property. Family, friends, and work associates are always looking for new investment opportunities and can help you grow your reputation as a lender. Starting with a few quality deals from inside your personal network will help you expand to other investors. If you're on the fence about whether to get into lending or not, starting small with a family member might be a good trial run. At the same time, friends and colleagues can present valuable connections from their own networks which can help you secure future deals.

Marketing is another route you can use to prepare yourself to become a private lender. Assess whether you have the resources for a marketing campaign. This ranges from taking out ad space and hiring an agent to starting websites and posting your resume. Get your name out there and start tracking your deals through a blog or social media—people will line up to take out a loan from you. But if you're unable to market yourself, or lack a network, private real estate lending might not be for you. It's not enough to merely have experience in the industry. Other people have to know about your experience. There has to be buzz about you.

The next thing you'll have to do is negotiate. It would be risky to get into private real estate lending before honing your negotiation skills. A large part of good negotiation is in the preparation. How do your proposed rates stack up against those of other lenders and banks in the same market? This type of research will also help you judge whether your net worth is high enough to engage in this type of passive investing. The more numbers you have at your disposal, either from prior real estate experience or from research and expert evaluations, the better prepared you'll be to seal up some high-quality private lending deals.

Report Card: Private Real Estate Lending

Time Commitment: Moderate

Being a private real estate lender is much less time consuming than active real estate investing. But this is definitely not a 'set-it-and-forget-it' investment either. You'll have to allocate time to research deals and meet with your team to analyze potential investors. Plus, you'll be pulled into numerous high-intensity negotiation sessions to settle the terms of your loans. Once the deal is inked you can theoretically kick back and enjoy regular disbursements, but you still ought to check in frequently to ensure your borrowers are hitting their deadlines and not overspending. Vigilance will help alert you to red flags and signs that a deal might be sour.

Dealflow: Moderate

Don't expect a surge of deal flow when you first get started, there is a lot of competition out there for private lenders. You might have to get your boots on the ground to chase leads, introduce friends to deals, or create a marketing campaign. Once you have a solid reputation, the deal flow is great. And unlike many other types of investments, these ones actually come to you. But it can take a few years of hard work to get to that point.

Capital Commitment: High

As you know, real estate deals are no small commitment. You'll likely be doling out anywhere from $150,000 to $500,000+ on every loan you make. And if you really want to pursue this passive income vehicle, you'll probably have to spread your risk across a few separate loans and manage them all simultaneously. To reiterate: *do not get into private real estate lending if you think you'd be wiped out by a single loan defaulting.*

Knowledge Requirement: High

Analyzing real estate markets takes a massive knowledge base. It significantly benefits you as a lender to have expertise in real estate before trying your hand at private real estate loans. However, you can always outsource the required knowledge by hiring experts to serve an advisory role. Generally speaking, you'd be taking a huge risk to lend a borrower your capital without sufficient knowledge of the market, rehab costs, and potential hurdles along the way.

Return Potential (ROI): High

Sitting at close to 10%, the average interest rates on private real estate loans present amazing return potential. You shouldn't consider a private loan with an interest rate under 5%. With the decent amount of time you will have to spend analyzing borrowers and deals, the interest rate should be worth your while. Overall, an interest rate between 9% to 15% is seldom found in other modes of passive income and so private real estate lending should be regarded as one of the best options out there.

Risk Level: High

A lot can go wrong on a private real estate loan. Foreclosure, defaults, underestimated costs—the list goes on. The risk level is high in this sector because when they come, the losses are devastating, and bad deals are common. While active real estate investing is thought to be riskier than lending, the amount of money at stake is just as high and a loss can do serious damage to your portfolio if you aren't well diversified.

Upside: Low

If the property your borrower purchases appreciates considerably or nets a sizable profit on its sale, you aren't really going to see any of that money. In some cases, you might ask for a small piece of the profits on sale, but this isn't typically the case. The terms of the loan are generally static and you'll be earning just as much as you expect: 10% (unless your borrower incurs fees). Much like investing in a savings account or CD, there isn't a lot of upside potential.

The Bottom Line

For those with ample net worth and experience in the industry, becoming a private lender to real estate developers and builders can make for big profits. It's difficult to find double-digit interest rates in any sector and this asset class comes with the added benefit of a physical asset—the property itself—to back your loan. Of course, that doesn't guarantee you won't lose money on a bad deal, but it helps. To improve your odds at turning a profit, a lot of research is required.

If you like the idea of real estate investing but think private lending sounds like too much work and risk, you might be a prime candidate for real estate investment trusts (REITs). I'll cover those in the next chapter. We'll start by talking about the implications of an important bill signed in 1960 by my favorite U.S. president—but first...

Video Assignment #7: Inside of "Family Offices"

This chapter, we explored private real estate lending and how, unless you're in a certain income or net worth bracket, it won't yield significant results. This is why real estate lending is often managed by family offices.

What exactly are family offices? You'll find out in this video. Family offices might be called offices, but they are actually financial vehicles used by the ultra-wealthy to keep their money safe for generations to come. Family offices tend to allocate a significant portion of their portfolio to commercial real estate.

To access the video, go to passiveincomethebook.com/7.

CHAPTER 8

Real Estate Investment Trusts

There are many things we can thank President Dwight D. Eisenhower for, such as our nation's critical infrastructure and the Interstate Highway System—which experts say we would be crippled as a nation without. Another Eisenhower White-House accomplishment was the founding of NASA in 1958. He was the first president to get America excited about the race to outer space. While those are both well and good, my personal favorite is a bill he signed into law which has allowed me to generate tens of millions of dollars in passive income for myself and my clients.

Eisenhower's biggest accomplishment, as far as I'm concerned, involved the type of investment fund known as a "Massachusetts Trust," which was popular throughout the 19th century as a way for wealthy individuals to avoid double taxation. Members of these trusts paid income tax on any money they personally made, but Massachusetts Trusts weren't considered corporations and were free from the grasp of corporate taxes (so long as the trust's income was entirely disbursed to its beneficiaries). It was a popular setup that allowed America's richest families to build incredible amounts of passive income. However, the "nothing good ever lasts" truism once again came true.

Amid the Great Depression of the 1930s, the Supreme Court ruled that a Massachusetts Trust was no longer exempt from corporate taxes. Under the new ruling, these trusts were suddenly subjected to hefty taxation on any and all profits made. Then, the same money was taxed again as personal income when it was distributed to shareholders. Investors were furious. Many hired lobbyists to pound on legislators' doors, demanding the double taxation law be overturned. For 30 long years these lobbyists fought until the decade of free love, televised elections, and civil rights movements rolled around. Finally, in the Fall of 1960, my favorite President, Dwight D. Eisenhower, stepped up and signed the Real Estate Investment Trust Act into law.

It was September 14th, 1960, when a single presidential pen stroke amended the law, officially classifying real estate investment trusts (REITs) as "pass-through entities." This meant REITs now qualified for corporate tax exemption if 90% of their taxable income was disbursed to shareholders. The investment community rejoiced and real estate barons gathered to pop bottles of champagne on the Senate steps. Okay that last part isn't true, but I have a feeling investors went home that Wednesday evening to enjoy a special pour on the rocks.

So, what are REITs exactly, and how did they transform into the wildly popular passive investment vehicles they are today?

REITs are entities required by the IRS to return at least 90% of their taxable income to shareholders (with many returning 100%). This means the payouts are generally quite good for the average investor. REITs generate income by purchasing and leasing property assets of all types including residential, commercial, and industrial buildings and structures.

Most REITs focus on a specific property class, but some diversify across office spaces, apartments, hotels, medical facilities, storage facilities, timberlands, retail centers, cell towers, and infrastructure to name a few. Some of the more popular property types are retail spaces, offices, health care facilities, and infrastructure, although all asset combinations are available and viable.

A significant advantage of REITs, as with other private trusts, is that investors gain the resources of a professional management team. Directors of REITs are generally seasoned experts in their specific property class and will do all of the work to hunt out good deals, renovate properties, and hire property managers. Thus, REITs are truly passive in a way that the previously discussed forms of real estate investing are not.

The goal of any REIT is to maximize shareholder value in order to attract more investors and purchase even more property. When a REIT's management team is able to sell one or more of their properties for a profit, those gains must be distributed back to the shareholders by law. In this way, REITs can provide both regular distributions as well as the potential for significant upside—a combination we haven't seen yet from any of the previous asset classes.

However, there are different types of REITs and not all of them are created equal.

First, there are publicly traded REITs. Shares in these can be bought and sold directly on the open stock exchange just like any other public security. Some of the big names include Simon Property Group (NYSE: SPG), Crown Castle International (NYSE: CCI), Public Storage (NYSE: PSA), and Prologis (NYSE: PLD). Like dividend stocks, public REITs offer a set distribution per share. This can be divided into the current share price to determine the yield. Typically, you can expect a publicly traded REIT to yield a healthy 4-5% per year.

The main issue with public REITs that limits their usefulness as passive income vehicles is the fact that their share price is determined by market forces. You might see an article about a fantastic REIT in *The Wall Street Journal* and decide to pick up a few thousand shares. Now you're all set to sit back and collect 5% per year! Except, what you failed to account for is that the price of this security was temporarily inflated due to the influx in demand generated by the WSJ piece. Over the next few months, after you click the 'buy' button, you'll watch the price slide back down by 20%.

Public REITs are subject to stock market volatility. And this volatility is completely irrational. Logically, the value of a REIT should never change. Every fund owns a certain amount of property with a certain fixed dollar value. These are tangible assets. The fund also has a certain cash flow every month that doesn't change. It seems counter to the facts that the price would wildly fluctuate.

The bottom line is share price vacillates because of market forces. Irrational investors are out there selling and buying shares which artificially inflates and deflates demand.

When you invest in public REITs you might lock in a guaranteed 4-5% ticket payment. But that doesn't do you much good if you lose 20% of your principal in the process. When the stock market drops, so will the value of your public REIT portfolio—even though the assets held by the fund haven't actually changed at all.

Mortgage REITs, or mREITs, operate by purchasing or originating mortgages and mortgage-backed securities on real estate. They make their income from the interest on mortgage investments, backed by tangible, income-generating properties. Like many equity REITs, mREITs are publicly traded and subject to market volatility. Also, they tend to provide slightly lower returns than equity REITs.

The final type of REIT is the private REIT. These funds function much like public REITs, purchasing properties, renovating them, finding tenants and managers, selling for a gain, and distributing all profit back to shareholders. However, unlike public REITs, private funds are not subject to market volatility. No, that is not a typo. The value of a private REIT is fixed. It is calculated based on the value of the underlying property held by the fund. The only way for the fund to lose value is for the property to substantially depreciate. However, like any REIT, these funds are usually managed by savvy real estate veterans with teams of analysts, accountants, and lawyers at their disposal. These people are pros.

With a privately traded REIT you can expect to make 6-8% returns on your capital every single year. Also, unlike publicly traded funds where you have to sell your shares and hope the irrational market has magically pushed the value up since you bought in, private REITs generally come with an exit plan included. The goal of the fund is to not only to return 7% of your money every single year, but also to turn a hefty profit for shareholders when the fund closes out. And, just like public REITs, private real estate funds are also required by law to distribute at least 90% of the gains accrued directly to their shareholders.

Here's what this would typically look like at my investment firm, Four Peaks Partners. When you buy into one of our funds, you sign up for a fixed period of time, just as you would with a corporate or government bond. Most of our funds have a duration of seven years. This means we collect a certain amount of money from investors like you—maybe $100 million total—to purchase a specific type of property—say, warehouses outside of Baton Rouge, Louisiana. Once the money has been raised, my team and I invest the $100 million to purchase and renovate a group of warehouses. Then, we hire a management team and quickly fill the spaces with tenants.

With the rent generated from these leases, we are able to immediately begin providing you and the rest of the investors a 7-8% return, paid quarterly. During the seven years the fund is active we work hard to renovate and improve the properties, enhancing their profitability. Then when the fund closes out we sell the warehouses for a profit and return all the money we earn back to investors. You might receive 150-175% of your principal back in addition to the 7-8% you've been earning every year.

Also, private REITs now provide a great tax benefit called a "pass-through deduction," which just became law in 2017 as a part of the Tax Cuts and Jobs Act (TCJA). This allows REIT investors to deduct up to 20% of their dividends, which is essentially tax-free money courtesy of Uncle Sam. If you're in the top tax bracket, this means the tax on your dividends could go from 37% down to 29.6%. For example, a $10,000 disbursement would be reduced to $8,000. Instead of paying $3,700 in taxes on the $10,000, you would have to pay $2960. In other words, pass-through deduction reduces the taxes you pay on dividends by over 7%. It's an amazing deal.

And remember, *REITs are not taxed at the corporate level*. This means REIT investors are only taxed once. This is a major reason why private REITs are the most popular savings vehicle among the top passive income investors.

However, because these funds are not publicly traded, they don't have to disclose their financials to non-investors. Also, most prefer to accept only accredited investors and generally require a minimum contribution of $100k-$1m. Finding the right REIT to invest in, where the team behind the fund is experienced and honest, is critical.

Next, I'll explore how to find the REIT that's perfect for you. And I'll show you exactly what to say on your application to make sure you'll be accepted by even the most competitive funds.

Picking the Perfect REIT for Passive Income

Sifting through the options to find the perfect REIT takes a good deal of time, effort, and patience. You typically don't want to rush the process, especially because the more advantageous private funds will generally have a term of 5-10 years during which you can't withdraw your money. Choosing the wrong one means you'll be locked up in a sub-standard asset for a significant stretch of time.

The upside of REITs compared to the other types of real estate invest-ments we've looked at is that with REITs you only have to do the work once. Then you never have to think about your investment again until the fund matures and you get your money back. It's completely passive. Because of this, it's worth it to do some serious research upfront before investing in one.

For publicly traded REITs, you can find all of their financial information and a complete list of their holdings without much digging. They are required to file these by law. This makes your job easier as you try to research the fund, which is nice. However, it also makes it difficult for the fund to consistently find undervalued properties to buy. As soon as they start investing in any market sector, they have to immediately report what they are doing, and competitors can swoop in and start buying up similar properties in the area. Doing business with this level of transparency is like if Coca-Cola had to share their secret formula with Pepsi and all the other soda companies.

Many public REITs (15-20%) invest in retail. In fact, retail space represents the single biggest investment type in America. Whatever shopping center you frequent, it's likely owned by a REIT. So, it could be a safe investment. But, then again, malls are dying. Business is moving online. Covid-19 hit the owners of these large public spaces hard. The chances that a mall will appreciate significantly in value are slim to none. Because public REITs have no "close out" date, they never have to worry about selling their properties for a profit. In fact, depreciation is great for their balance sheet as it can be written off. No wonder why so many of them are investing in retail!

Private REITs, on the other hand, seek to purchase properties with the potential to significantly appreciate over the coming years. This means they might focus on distressed or recovering markets where properties can be had for a low price relative to their actual value. That means Beverly Hills is out. Same with Park Place and Haight Ashbury. Don't expect savvy private REITs to be investing in properties that are sexy or glamorous. In fact, the opposite is generally true. Look for these types of funds to be pouring investment dollars into the seedy part of town; neighborhoods on the verge of being home to an art scene and a new Starbucks...you know, places that are about to gentrify. That's where the upside is. And with private REITs upside matters...a lot.

The difficult thing about these funds is the secrecy. They aren't going to be posting their new properties proudly on their website for all to see. The people who run private REITs don't want to advertise their strategies because they don't want to attract other investors to their markets and start getting outbid on new properties. The types of properties they buy and the geographic areas they focus on are trading secrets that they've worked hard to discover ahead of everyone else.

Notice how I haven't actually mentioned what types of properties my fund focuses on. This isn't an accident. I referred to warehouses outside of Baton Rouge, Louisiana above. But that's not what we really do. If you want to learn what we are currently doing with our capital, you'll have to invest in one of our funds. And our minimum contribution is $100,000. A pretty steep price of admission just to learn what we're up to.

This secrecy makes it difficult to compare REITs and decide which one to invest in.

What you have to do is apply to a few different funds and go through their screening process. This is time and energy intensive so it's best to do as much research as you can beforehand and only approach your top few choices. The screening process will usually involve an introductory call to make sure you really want to invest and aren't just trying to steal secrets. For this, it actually helps if you aren't an active real estate investor yourself. REITs don't like to admit other investors unless they agree to sign a non-compete. And even then it could be touch-and-go. If you have real estate experience, downplay it on the initial call. Aim to come across as a wealthy individual who wants to diversify with real estate, but doesn't have the time or energy to actively invest.

Private REITs, including Four Peaks Partners, love people like this.

Doctors. Lawyers. Entrepreneurs. Politicians. Software engineers. Retired people. Anyone who is successful and has capital to invest, but doesn't look like a threat. If this sounds like you, there's a good chance you can sail right through the initial screening call and find yourself on a second call with the fund manager to discuss your potential investment. You need to be honest and tell this person that you are trying to choose between three different possible funds. Ask them what they can tell you about their "secret sauce" and their past results. By law, these people cannot lie about previous performance when you ask them a direct question. But they can choose not to answer if they feel you are prying too deeply into their trade secrets.

Ask about the annual rate of return they can guarantee. If it's less than 6%, *run*. If it's over 9% that's also a sign something shady might be going on. Get some numbers for the last few funds the firm has closed out on. What kind of upside did investors see? What fees were assessed and how much did the average investor take home? They can tell you this over the phone, but they don't like to put it in writing because that makes it easy to share. If you need to, take notes on your calls for easy comparison between your options.

Another thing to watch out for is over-diversification. A good REIT should have a focused strategy and should stick to a narrow slice of the market in which they have extreme expertise. As they say, a jack of all trades is a master of none. If you ask about the fund's "secret sauce" and the partner starts talking about diversifying across various markets and property types, that's a red flag. A fund with a wide range of property types will yield average returns at best.

You want to find a REIT where the team specializes in a narrow type of real estate. The best funds will sound almost too weirdly niche and specific to the average investor.

1. "We buy strip clubs in the suburbs of Chicago."

2. "This fund focuses on buying up solar energy farms in the New Mexico desert."
3. "Our next REIT will be targeting single-family homes in small Midwestern towns."

Believe it or not, those are great answers. The more oddly specific the focus of the fund is, the more likely you are to see a huge upside on your investment—in addition to cushy returns year-over-year. One caveat here is that the team behind the fund needs to have some actual expertise in the niche they've decided to target. Have they managed a previous fund in a similar market with a successful exit? If not, keep looking. A high-quality team is everything when you're buying into a private REIT.

Most economists emphasize that you'll get the highest gains on any investment if you leave your money alone as long as possible without touching it. The beauty of privately held REITs is that they actually force you to do this. You can't withdraw your money until the fund closes out. Your money is used to buy properties and those properties have to be sold before you can cash out. Because of this, it's always best to leave the timing of the sale up to the fund managers. Private REITs ensure this. But with public REITs, investors can sell their shares any time they want. At the first sign of a downturn in the real estate market, people bail out and sell, driving the price down and causing millions of dollars in value to disappear.

Don't be afraid to sign up for five to ten years, but do your homework before committing. There's no need to rush. Watch your basket closely, before and after you put your eggs in it.

I hope you're feeling good about your options for this type of passive investing. It doesn't require any active work once you choose a fund to invest in. It's 100% passive and the returns are mouth-wateringly good. Now let's talk about when it might be a good time for you to invest in the REIT market.

Tips for Sophisticated Investors

A REIT is a long-term passive income investment, which means that no matter when you buy into one of these funds the annual return is always going to be the same. That's great news. You don't have to try to time your investments based on market conditions. Once you find a good fund with a solid team behind it, go for it.

When a REIT closes out at the end of five to ten years, you'll notice a difference in upside depending on what happened in the real estate market during the intervening period. If the market is up from where it was when you bought in, you'll see a bigger upside. If the market has dropped, your upside will be smaller. However, if the team managing your fund is competent you should never lose money. At Four Peaks Partners, even in turbulent market conditions, our funds have always been able to turn a profit for our investors.

One recommendation I can make is to invest in a new REIT every year for seven years, creating a REIT ladder. This way, once the first fund closes out you'll have a new flood of cash coming your way every year to re-invest in a new fund. Thanks to the hefty upsides, you'll be growing your principle while still making impressive yearly returns. The big benefit with this approach is that some seven-year stretches will simply provide more favorable market conditions than others. If you buy into a new fund every year, you'll be sure to benefit from the big market swings which can occasionally spell returns of 200% or more. Whereas if you just invest all of your capital in one fund every seven years, you might miss out one of the best times to invest.

Another key is to have your accountant or lawyer set up an LLC or personal trust for you to hold your REITs in. This way you can reinvest your entire windfall back into a new REIT every year without paying capital gains tax on your upside. That's a huge advantage.

Because private REITs do not fluctuate with the stock market, they are a fantastic addition to a regular stock portfolio and can be held in a tax-sheltered retirement account if that's something you have available.

I would also advise against purchasing many different REITs at one time. The more diversified your investments get, the closer your returns will be to average. You don't want to be average when it comes to your passive income.

One final thing to keep an eye on when it comes to REITs is the Federal Funds Rate. You should already be keeping track of this every week if you paid attention to Chapter 2 and Chapter 3 on bonds and savings vehicles. It also plays an important role in the real estate world because low-interest rates mean more investors will be able to get loans and purchase real estate, driving up prices in the coming years. Therefore, when interest rates are low many investors start swarming around REITs like a cloud of locusts. When interest rates are low it's the absolute best time to invest in a real estate fund. On the contrary, high-interest rates can make REITs more unpredictable.

Real estate is one of the best ways to start earning serious passive cash flow, and REITs make it easy for anybody to get involved. You'll have experts working hard to make you money while you sit back. Active investors and lenders can make more, but also require more work, and not everyone wants to get their hands dirty. REITs can save you the headache while still making you rich.

Report Card: Real Estate Investment Trust (REIT)

Time Commitment: Low

Purchasing publicly traded REITs is as simple as buying stocks. It takes almost no time at all. You might spend a few hours researching the best type of REIT for you and deciding which asset class you want to focus on. That's about it. Private REITs require a bit more work to select the right one. Information is harder to obtain because they don't want other investors stealing their secrets and competing with them in their niche markets. Once you choose a fund and make your investment, it's 100% passive. Your money might be locked up for a certain amount of time depending on the deal, but you won't have to lift a finger in order to collect your checks.

Dealflow: High

REITs are becoming an increasingly popular investment opportunity and you'll always have the chance to invest. Whether public or private, real estate investment trusts are competing for your investment. One caveat is that some private REITs require investors to be accredited, which can narrow your deal flow if you aren't there yet. Get accredited as soon as possible to widen the field of options.

Capital Commitment (Private): Moderate

If you're going the private route, don't be surprised by a $25,000 minimum. You'll probably be able to find companies that are willing to take as little as $10,000 and offer liquidity in some form, but I wouldn't call that the "norm." At Four Peaks Partners, we require a minimum contribution of $100,000 and some investments ask for half a million or a million dollars to get started.

Capital Commitment (Public): Low

When it comes to public REITs you can invest as little as the cost of a single share. The price per share has a wide range, but it won't put a big dent in your wallet. Some of the largest public REITs cost around $80 per share on average, so you can get started exploring the benefits of a REIT investment for the price of a higher-end bottle of wine. These also come with the added advantage of liquidity. You can sell your shares in a public REIT whenever you want (and many people do just that—causing the price to fluctuate wildly for no apparent reason).

Knowledge Requirement: Low

Perhaps the biggest benefit of a REIT is that you don't have to know what you're doing. You'll have a team of experts on your side! REIT managers, directors, and trustees work hard to make the most of your investment dollars, so you don't need to be a real estate expert to start earning impressive returns. The knowledge required is simple: research companies with the best track record. After the fund closes out and your principal is returned, you'll have to decide whether to reinvest with the same firm again or try your capital somewhere else.

Return Potential (ROI): Moderate to High

REIT returns are not the ultra-high 12% you might see as a private lender, but REITs are much more lucrative than a 2% savings bond. With rates of about 7% on average, your return is comparable to investing in the stock market, and might even be better, as many REITs return close to 9%. Considering the low time and knowledge commitment, a 7-8% interest rate is impressive. Plus, thanks to my favorite president, REITs are taxed only once and shareholders can benefit from a handful of other tax breaks like the pass-through deduction benefit (courtesy of the Trump administration).

Risk Level: Moderate

Public REITs are not immune to stock market volatility. Their share price can fluctuate significantly based solely on demand and the news cycle. At the end of the day, REIT investments are backed by physical real estate assets, which makes them less risky than more speculative investments in private equity or venture capital. Even if your REIT experiences depreciation of their assets, you might still be okay as an investor because you can write it all off as a "loss" and you won't have to pay as high of a tax on "return of capital."

Upside: Moderate

Real estate is known for its high appreciation potential, and as REITs grow you can get a nice piece of the upside. This is especially true in the private sector where funds close out and return all of the profits directly to shareholders. However, most established public REITs don't experience significant growth because they already own a vast, diversified portfolio of properties. Because of this, their upside potential is diminished compared to private REITs or public funds that have opened recently.

The Bottom Line

You can stand to earn significant passive income from REITs and you don't have to become an expert on real estate to cash in. This passive investment vehicle is widely popular and seems to be growing, despite the 2008 financial crisis. There's a great variety of REITs to explore and the returns are good, without costing you much time at all. I really like REITs for these reasons—and so do my clients.

The main drawback to REITs for many newer investors is the high minimum contributions. If you want to experience the benefits of a REIT without putting up $100k, crowdfunding real estate platforms might be the ticket. I'll cover those in the next chapter. But first, how New York City almost lost its iconic Statue of Liberty because they ran out of room.

Video Assignment #8: Use REITs for Generational Wealth

In this video, we'll explore using REITs to build generational wealth. With regular disbursements and a strong potential for appreciation, REITs are an ideal vehicle to build generational wealth. Pay attention to the leverage levels of a fund. Leverage results in more interest going out, reducing earnings to investors.

To access the video, go to passiveincomethebook.com/8.

CHAPTER 9

Crowdfunding Real Estate

The best investment opportunities usually require you to be an accredited investor with a minimum contribution of $100,000 to $1 million, but there is a way for smaller, non-accredited investors to get in on the action: crowdfunding. There is a growing movement in the investing community toward decentralized lending and it is creating opportunities for even the smallest investors. Crowdfunding has been catching on quickly during the past few years thanks to technology, but the practice actually dates back to the year 1885, when New York City had a big problem: there was nowhere to put the Statue of Liberty.

The entire metropolis was in turmoil because citizens knew the copper monument was scheduled to arrive from France. But the city was running short on funds and couldn't spare the cash to construct a large concrete base to support Lady Liberty. New Yorkers couldn't bear the thought of the shining statue guarding the gates of Philadelphia, or worse, rival city Boston. No way in hell. New York City wanted the colossal Roman goddess of freedom in *their* hometown.

Joseph Pulitzer, renowned journalist, publisher, and namesake for the prestigious Pulitzer Prize, connected the dots and realized mass media could solve this problem. He leveraged the platform of his newspaper, the

New York World, to solicit donations directly from individual New Yorkers in order to finish construction of the pedestal. New Yorkers are notoriously proud, competitive, and stubborn and Pulitzer had a hunch that the people of the city would pitch in to prevent their statue from going somewhere else.

It turns out Pulitzer was right. Citizens decided to take the matter into their own hands. Over 160,000 donors sent in their hard-earned money to secure the placement of the Statue of Liberty in New York City. Without fully realizing it, Pulitzer had tapped into the immense power of crowdfunding. With this practice, large amounts of capital can be raised in small increments. In the case of the Statue of Liberty, 90% of donations that came in were for a single dollar. It was not a few wealthy patrons but, rather, the combined effort of tens of thousands that made the impossible possible. The masses spoke. And their voices were heard, loud and clear.

Despite this tremendous feat, however, crowdfunding as a business model did not gain real traction for another 100 years. The big reason for the recent explosion in crowdfunding is, as you might guess, the advent of the internet. Previously, crowdfunding efforts relied on mass media outlets like the newspaper, radio, and television. This meant it might have been a viable model for media moguls like Joseph Pulitzer, politicians, and already-famous artists, but for the average individual it was out of reach.

Today there are numerous online platforms that allow anyone with a big idea to raise money directly from individual investors and donors.

In 1997, an online crowdfunding campaign was used to put rock and roll on the road. British band Marillion was able to raise $60,000 in donations to tour the U.S. Apparently the band's fans agreed that the show must go on—and they were willing to pony up the cash to make it happen. This fundraiser broke the mold and paved the way for a new industry in digital crowdfunding, inspiring online entrepreneurs everywhere to jump on the bandwagon.

It didn't take long for musician and computer programmer Brian Camelio to recognize the untapped potential of online crowdfunding. He launched the first online company to take advantage of this model in 2001, a site called ArtistShare, where musicians and performers could crowdsource funding for creative projects. ArtistShare's first successfully financed project was **Concert in a Garden**, a jazz album from Maria Schneider. The album was released in 2004 and won the Grammy award for best large jazz ensemble album in 2005. For the next three years, ArtistShare albums would consistently take home Grammy Awards. This remarkable feat showed the world that online crowdfunding was a viable way to fund and promote new projects in a variety of industries while turning a profit at the same time.

And these award-winning albums weren't even sold in stores. The only way to get your hands on **Concert in a Garden** in 2004 was to contribute $9.95 or more to Maria's project in exchange for an electronic download of the finished project. Donors contributing $250 had their names added to the album's credits. One fan who donated over $10,000 was listed as an executive producer.

This tiered system of donations became a trend in the world of online crowdfunding (particularly in the arts) as the industry exploded and gained billions in capital from a majority of small donations. Indiegogo launched in 2008 and has raised $1.6 billion from 11 million people with 19,000 new projects every month. Kickstarter began in 2009 and has raised $4.79 billion, funding over 476,000 projects with a success rate of 38%. GoFundMe, established in 2010, has raised $5 billion from 50 million backers over 2 million campaigns.

You might be familiar with one of the most outlandish Kickstarter campaigns: the Pebble smartwatch. Three years before the launch of the Apple Watch, entrepreneurs from Palo Alto, California, sought $100,000 in donations to create a smartwatch that could interface with iPhone and

Android phones and run apps for health and fitness. Those who pledged $115 would receive a Pebble watch, which was much cheaper than the planned retail price. Those providing greater contributions would earn higher tiers of awards, such as two Pebble watches for a mere $220. Within 2 hours of launch, Pebble had reached its goal of $100,000. A month later, Pebble ended their Kickstarter campaign with over $10 million in funding.

However, it's important to point out that receiving funding doesn't mean a project will necessarily be fulfilled. About 70% of Kickstarter campaigns are late to deliver—if they deliver at all. To date, the platform does not step in to handle these issues, and backers can be left empty-handed after making an investment. The biggest downside to using online platforms to fund entrepreneurial projects seems to be the high prevalence of this 'take-the-money-and-run' approach. Most crowdfunded investments are not backed by tangible assets, contracts, or guarantees that the sites hosting these projects will intervene to ensure investors get what they were promised. (However, if a project does not reach its funding goal, some sites will refund contributors' donations.)

This is less of a concern when it comes to crowdfunding real estate. With the increasing prevalence of crowdfunding opportunities on the web, the real estate industry is starting to dip its toes in too. The benefit for investors is that a willingness to be held accountable is paramount to real estate crowdfunds. In order to attract investors, real estate crowdfunding companies work hard to show that their service includes built-in accountability. These investment opportunities are similar to private REITs, except the nature of crowdfunding allows each investor to pledge a smaller amount. This makes it a great low-barrier way to get started in real estate investing without needing much capital.

Compared with some of the other types of lending I have discussed, like private equity and secured private real estate lending, crowdfunding is much easier to get started with because the minimum contribution is many orders of magnitude lower. There is also a much broader range of opportunities available. Many online funding platforms are open to any investor with as little as $100 to spend. Others require investors to be accredited or to meet minimum investment requirements. Nonetheless, on the whole, these platforms allow virtually anyone to participate in asset classes that offer high risk-adjusted returns without a huge capital outlay. If you want to invest in real estate without purchasing or developing a property, then becoming a shareholder through a real estate crowdfunding platform might be for you.

Although real estate crowdfunding makes up a small percentage of commercial and residential real estate deals in the U.S., it does appear to be gaining momentum. There are more real estate crowdfunding platforms popping up every day and the multibillion-dollar industry is expanding.

If you decide to invest in this passive income vehicle you can expect reasonably high returns. For a small initial investment, you can earn 7-13% per year based on historical data. With this vehicle, you can invest in a private fund that offers you the opportunity to reap the income, appreciation, and security benefits of commercial real estate investing and secured private lending without the headaches. There are low minimum investments and, in most cases, no investor qualification requirements for crowdsourced funds. However, this asset class isn't without issues and risks to be aware of.

What Could Go Wrong?

Real estate crowdfunding is a popular emerging investment opportunity, but there are some major drawbacks you should be aware of before you consider it. The first thing to keep in mind with crowdfunding platforms is that they aren't looking for qualified investors. Anyone with $100 can get involved. You don't need to be accredited or even have an ID. These websites function more like startups than traditional investment funds. Their financial statements reveal they spend more on social media marketing than on due diligence for the deals on their platforms.

In fact, after you finish reading this book, don't be surprised if ads for real estate crowdfunding platforms start to follow you around the internet. The digital marketing teams for these sites spend millions on ads every year to attract new investors to the platform. All of this advertising, of course, isn't free. And that means they have to charge fees after you invest to recoup their marketing budget. These sites are masters at hiding fees. You might notice fundraising fees, management fees, performance-related fees, and transaction-based fees all being stealthily assessed to your account. These are in addition to fees charged to the developer.

The structure of these fees varies from one company to another, but it is important to understand that investors always pay in some way. The advertising isn't free. The sites cost a lot of money to build and run. The fees come in various forms and will absolutely need to be factored into your analysis before you decide to contribute to any crowdfunding platform.

Marketing campaigns are the bread and butter of crowdsourcing platforms. Their business model involves finding massive quantities of small-time backers instead of a few investors with deep pockets. In this way, crowdsourcing platforms spend at least as much on marketing as legal fees, which can quickly add up to hundreds of thousands per month.

The good news is your investment won't be held by the crowdfunding platform for long. Once the project is funded, the capital raised will go into a single LLC that manages the property and pays out disbursements to investors. This means even if the platform goes bankrupt before the project is complete, your investment will usually be safe. Later on, I'll show you a case study from a company called RealtyShares that paints this picture perfectly.

But first, we need to address the common aggressive marketing campaigns crowdfunding platforms often stoop too. Some people may be wondering if they are even legal, and it's been debated whether they are trustworthy or just bait for suckers. Spying on consumers is definitely a gray area today, and while many people are repulsed by this common practice I have a feeling it's not going away any time soon. In fact, massive investing campaigns are perfectly legal in the United States.

It all comes back to the JOBS (Jumpstart Our Business Startups) Act of 2008. The most revolutionary component of this bill was that it allowed small and mid-sized companies to advertise their opportunities to people who might not come across them otherwise. Following the JOBS Act, the SEC lifted restrictions on non-accredited investors, allowing anyone to invest in crowdfunding for private equity and real estate.

Crowdfunding makes it easy for anyone to get involved, as their advertisements boast, and the minimums can be anywhere from $100 to $1,000 depending on the platform. Not too shabby if you want to take a risk on a relatively new and unproven passive vehicle, but you don't want to risk your whole nest egg. You can even spread out a few $100 contributions across multiple funds or platforms to test which models and asset classes earn you the greatest returns.

In fact, when it comes to crowdfunding, diversification is probably a good idea.

Wait a minute. If you're reading carefully, you've probably noticed that I am strongly against diversification. I quoted some of the most successful investors of all time, like Warren Buffett, who said, "Diversification is protection against ignorance. It only makes sense for investors who don't know what they are doing." And Andrew Carnegie said, "Put all your eggs in one basket and then watch that basket."

But when it comes to crowdfunding, I'm changing my tune because crowdfunding is, quite simply, a crapshoot. When you invest using these platforms, you are taking a risk on a company that is fairly unknown. They don't have a lot of financial history to back up their potential or their promises. And this is a rapidly changing industry, which means no single platform is reliable. In the past year alone, 13 of the top 25 crowdfunding sites have completely dropped out of the rankings. Many have entirely gone out of business. Due to the constant flux in this new industry, many companies are forced to adjust their business model on the fly, which can be either beneficial or catastrophic.

It's impossible to study an investment carefully, analyze the fundamentals, and be sure it's a good deal when you use a crowdfunding platform. You are given little to go on. Because the developer has to post information publicly on the internet, they don't reveal to you much about their plans, otherwise they would lose any competitive advantage they had. It's a bit like playing darts blindfolded. If you want a chance at scoring, you'd better throw a lot of darts.

That's why, in the case of crowdfunding, I recommend a high level of diversification if you're going to get involved. In fact, it's prudent to not only invest in multiple opportunities on a single platform, but to actually spread your investments out across numerous different platforms to get the broadest level of diversification possible.

Another factor to consider when investing in these deals is the possibility of delay on payments. Many crowdfunded ventures do not pay a fixed return based on your initial investment. The return depends on the profitability of the property and on how much revenue can be disbursed to investors after costs have been accounted for (including marketing costs). Most investors won't see any upsides on the property until the 'preferred returns' are paid. Sometimes, depending on the platform, you won't earn any interest at all until the property becomes cash flow positive, which can take anywhere from a few months to a few years.

As with any investment, the most important piece of the puzzle here is education. You need to learn how to vet sponsors and analyze deals. However, since there isn't a lot of financial information available on crowdfunding platforms, you operate with one hand tied behind your back. Some of the only metrics you'll have access to are the equity multiples for recent projects and the internal revenue rate (IRR) of the platform. A higher IRR usually means the investment can be profitable. But, of course, past success is no guarantee of future success, and when the platform has only existed for a few years, these numbers are fairly worthless.

Recently, RealtyShares, a large real estate crowdfunding platform, sent out a mass email to all of its constituents saying that the platform can no longer take on any new investors. This is interesting because the underlying real estate is still performing, and those who were able to put money into an LLC are still seeing some returns. The company, however, is floundering. Their management had critical flaws that are pushing them close to bankruptcy.

RealtyShares may yet recover, but the underlying problem they encountered in their business was scalability. RealtyShares grew too fast and couldn't scale up to meet the overflow of demand, leading them to shut their doors to new investments. The pie wasn't big enough to handle how many people wanted a slice. This kind of thing happens frequently in this industry. For this reason, among others I've mentioned, it's smart to spread out your minimum investments across a wide range of platforms. You never know when a growing company can go under, or when a newer company might take off and offer unexpected upsides.

Next, we'll cover when to dive into crowdsourcing and how to get started.

Is Real Estate Crowdfunding Right For You?

Maybe crowdfunding seems interesting to you based on what you've read in this chapter, but how do you know when it's the right time to get involved in this passive income vehicle? I think a good way to start is by comparing crowdfunding against traditional REITs. This will help you see the major pros and cons of investing.

First, there are many similarities between REITs and crowdfunding platforms. Both give investors an easy way to balance their portfolios and earn monthly passive income along with the potential for long-term appreciation on the underlying real estate assets. They also both provide the opportunity to invest in multiple real estate classes at once. You can spread your money around to different properties and even entirely different markets in different geographic areas, and this can help you avoid potential volatility in one specific market or another. Both are also indirect methods of investing, so you don't need to be an expert on real estate to get involved in either of these passive income vehicles.

One of the key advantages of REITs is that they offer the added bonus of professional opinions. When you invest in a private REIT, for example, you'll be working with sponsors who are experts in real estate and can talk you through the various prospects and navigate the risk/reward calculations. This knowledge is invaluable, especially when you don't have the time available to study the market or if you lack experience and connections in the industry. The beauty here is that when you find a team you trust, you'll be able to lean on your sponsor to help you execute your vision and you'll have top of the line consulting on your side. The cost for this service is baked into the firm's management fees.

With crowdfunding, on the other hand, you're on your own to decide what to do with your money. And you have little meaningful information to help you in your choice. You'll look through a library of "pre-approved" opportunities, watch a brief video advertising each one, and select whatever excites you the most. It's a bit like deciding which products to buy based on the quality of their television ads. You might pick a great one...or not.

With a REIT you won't be choosing the individual properties to buy for yourself, the management team will choose them for you based on a careful analysis of the market, financials, rehab costs, and rental projections. If you'd like to have more control over the individual properties you're investing in, crowdfunding might be a better option. But remember, those choices will be based on much more surface-level characteristics compared to the decisions your management team would be making at a REIT.

For the majority of investors who opt to go with crowdfunding over a traditional REIT, the deciding factor is usually cost. You can get started in crowdfunding for as little as $100. Whereas a historically successful REIT is going to have a minimum investment of $100,000 or more in order to join the fund. If you have enough capital, you're much better off going this route. However, crowdfunding is a great way to get started while you save up the money to join a REIT.

One thing to keep in mind is that there is a limit on how much you can legally invest using crowdfunding platforms. This law exists to protect investors because crowdfunding is highly speculative. If your annual income and net worth are greater than $107,000, you're allowed to invest up to 10% of your income or net worth over a 12-month period, as long as that investment does not exceed $107,000. If your income or net worth are less than $107,000, you can only invest 5%. That's another reason why I say crowdfunding is fine for dabbling and getting your feet wet in real estate, but it's not going to make you rich.

Remember, crowdfunding comes with risks—just like any type of investing. Most notably, you'll need to prepare for market volatility as well as potential defaults from developers. To make things more difficult, there is no secondary market to resell shares purchased from crowdsourcing platforms. This can greatly reduce liquidity. Once you're in, there's virtually no way to get out.

Also, generally you will need decent credit to get involved in most of the legitimate crowdfunding options. Don't get your hopes up for lots of opportunities if your finances aren't in order. Those with bad credit will likely be rejected by crowdfunding platforms.

Finally, real estate crowdsourcing should definitely be thought of as a long-term investment. As I explained in my last chapter, some offers don't pay out any interest or dividends until the property becomes profitable, which can take anywhere from a few months to a few years. The return potentially can be good once you eventually start making money, but it's often not clear when that will be.

Report Card: Real Estate Crowd Funding

Time Commitment: Low

It takes hardly any time at all to invest in real estate crowdfunding. All you have to do is register for your favorite platform, pass a basic credit check, link up a bank account, and start making investments. Because little information is provided about each investment, you won't have to spend a long time researching. In general, you will have to rely on the fact that every investment has been "pre-approved" by the platform's analysts.

Dealflow: High

Crowdfunding platforms are spreading like weeds. For every one that goes bankrupt and disappears, four or five new ones sprout up to take its place (and market share). There are no shortage of opportunities in this sector, which allows you to spread out your investments across multiple companies. Some will bear fruit and others will end up rotting in the field. Since there is so much competition in this relatively new arena of passive investing, there are thousands of companies trying to get your attention and rise to the top. Dealflow is the least of your worries, however, finding high-quality deals can be a challenge. Luckily, the minimums are extremely low compared to other real estate investment strategies, and the maximum investment is capped at 5% or 10% of your annual income. You'll never lose all of your money on one deal.

Capital Commitment: Low

Minimums are low. You can get started for a fraction of the cost of the majority of the sophisticated investing strategies. The goal of crowdfunding is to accumulate a massive amount of money from small contributions, so that no individual investor should ever have to pay an arm and a leg to get involved, or take on the lion's share of risk. In fact, it's illegal to invest more than 10% of your income in this asset class.

Knowledge Requirement: Low

The hardest part of your research is going to be vetting the quality of the fund or platform. Since there isn't going to be significant financial history, you won't have a lot to review. You don't need specialized knowledge to get started...but this can also leave you vulnerable to some potentially dangerous unknowns. Nonetheless, these funds claim to do all the real estate research for you and provide you with many options before you decide where to invest. You don't need expertise, and the platform is designed to be accessible to newcomers.

Return Potential (ROI): High

When these investments do pay, it's not unreasonable to expect a 7-13% return, which is great. It might not be as high as active, direct real estate investing or private lending, and it might not be as consistent and predictable as a REIT, but it's nothing to sneeze at considering the low cost, time, and knowledge requirements. The big thing to keep in mind is the risk involved.

Risk Level: High

In any real estate deal, there is a risk of default and poor market conditions that can eat up your investment. With crowdfunding, the risks are even greater because you're getting into a rapidly changing market with high volatility and turnover. There's a good chance any platform you use will be out of business by the time your investment matures.

Upside: Moderate

There's a chance that your underlying real estate assets can appreciate in value, but it's not guaranteed. Even if this does happen, you'll be one of the last people to get paid out after the developer covers all costs and debts incurred during the project and takes their fee for managing the deal. It's not uncommon for crowdfunded projects not to pay anything extra out on the sale of the property. They will return your initial money first and then give you a small cut of the proceeds if anything is left over.

The Bottom Line

Crowdsourcing can be good for small-time investors looking to get started in real estate. It is not demanding on the investor's time and offers relatively strong returns based on historical data. You have to watch out for shady platforms and the chance of default, but it also allows for easy diversification, which can allow you to hedge.

Next, I'll cover another hot topic in passive income investing: peer-to-peer lending. People email me all the time, asking if they can really make an easy 10% using this strategy. I'll break it down for you in the next chapter.

Video Assignment #9: Direct vs Indirect Investing

In the last two chapters, we've covered indirect methods of investing. For this chapter's video, I want to share a more detailed comparison of direct vs. indirect investing. While direct investments are often a more effective way to build wealth quickly, they require skills and a lot of hard work. To reduce volatility and protect your wealth for the long term, I recommend transitioning some of your portfolio to indirect investments.

To access the video, go to passiveincomethebook.com/9.

CHAPTER 10

Peer-to-Peer Lending

You might associate peer-to-peer lending with smartphone apps, but it actually dates back many thousands of years. Before there were banks, people made loans directly to each other. We may have Jonathan Swift to thank for pushing the idea of peer-to-peer loans into the mainstream over 100 years ago. In addition to his writings and political activism, the satirist and author of *Gulliver's Travels* is famous for his work in decentralized banking—or "peer lending." Throughout his life, Swift often loaned out small amounts to his struggling countrymen to help them get new businesses off the ground or purchase machinery or livestock to grow a venture. His core principles for success with peer lending were:

1. Screen borrowers for legitimacy

2. Be repaid in weekly increments

3. Have consignment rather than physical collateral

4. Involve the law and sue if a loan defaults

Many successful microcredit lenders today use similar strategies. The one thing that really separated Swift from the rest, however, was that he didn't charge interest. He was more interested in the 'social' portion of social lending than in trying to make a buck. At the end of the day, Swift wanted to change people's lives by helping them get on their feet financially. And he ultimately inspired Ireland to create a national loan fund system.

Throughout history, the popularity of peer lending has generally depended on the strength of the national banking system. When banks are weak or untrustworthy, more people make personal loans to each other. Whereas when banks are strong, borrowers are more likely to use the bank to finance their endeavors. This trend is very much alive today. For instance, peer lending grew rapidly following the 2008 financial crisis and the bankruptcy of Lehman Brothers. During this period, people had less faith in banks, but still needed loans. Thus, record numbers of Americans turned to peer lending.

Another factor that has led to an explosion in peer lending is the rise of the Internet, and the ease to find a willing peer to lend to you. In recent years, online platforms have been popping up left and right to make peer lending accessible to all. With the advent of these platforms, the industry has grown in leaps and bounds each year. These sites provide opportunities for lenders to connect with borrowers to obtain relatively small loans. This can be a life-changing opportunity for borrowers with poor credit who cannot get approval for a bank loan. Additionally, peer lending provides a promising stream of passive income for investors.

When one individual loans money to another via the internet, the transaction is known as peer-to-peer (P2P) lending. However, the practice also goes by the more general labels of "social lending" and "crowdlending." The online form of this passive income vehicle has only existed since 2005, but it has quickly erupted in popularity and numerous platforms have sprung up like Prosper, Lending Club, Funding Marketplace, Upstart, StreetShares, Zopa, RateSetter, and Peerform. The basic function of these sites is to connect those looking to borrow money with those looking to loan it out. This arrangement can, of course, be mutually beneficial and it dramatically simplifies and speeds up the process of borrowing and lending.

Many people who get involved in loaning money through a peer-to-peer platform do so purely for selfish reasons. After all, it's an easy way to make (potentially) above-market returns at around 10%. And, on some sites, the returns can go as high as 30% for lenders who are willing to take on riskier loans. Another attractive quality to this passive income stream is that it's socially rewarding. Peer-to-peer lending allows struggling individuals to escape from high-rate debt (like credit card debt) and to avoid bank loan denials. It's a way to make a positive impact on the community. Case in point, Jonathan Swift found peer lending so rewarding, he didn't charge any interest at all. He did it purely because he wanted to make a difference.

Of course, peer lending doesn't come without risks. The type of people who cannot get a quality bank loan and turn to peer lending might be those with poor credit history and low chances of paying the money back. In other words, you could be at risk of default. Data suggests that just 2% of peer-to-peer loans default, but that ratio can reach as high as 10% if you focus on high-yield loans to borrowers with bad credit history. Remember, peer-to-peer lending platforms are only there to connect borrowers and lenders. They aren't going to ride in like a knight in shining armor and repay you for a loan that goes south. Simply put, it's your risk, and it's your loss.

This is, perhaps, the biggest risk to consider if you decide to give social lending a try. On one hand, you could be really helping someone in need and your loan could have a major positive impact on their life—the potential to earn some passive income is a nice bonus. On the other hand, the higher default rate and elevated risk of peer-to-peer loans could completely wipe out your profits. It only takes one big loss to undo years of steady growth through peer-to-peer platforms.

And bad borrowers aren't the only risk in the world of peer-to-peer lending. You also need to watch out for the platforms themselves.

After the launch of the first online peer-to-peer platform, Zopa, in the

United Kingdom in 2005, many other countries started to explore the business model with mixed success. The United States, for instance, became interested in peer-to-peer platforms to the point where popular banks, like Wells Fargo, consider them a serious competitor. Other nations, such as Japan have outlawed online social lending platforms altogether.

The worst crisis in peer lending's short history has to be in China, where rampant fraud has left millions robbed of their savings. Hundreds of platforms were revealed to be 'shadow banks.' In fact, about half of all peer-to-peer platforms in the country are either under investigation or have simply closed up shop and run off with the capital investments. The billions of dollars in losses have been catastrophic. Single mothers and widows have lost their life savings in the hopes of getting a fair return on their capital. Some have been forced to sell their homes just to survive. There were even a number of ripped-off investors driven to suicide in shame.

The whole situation was shady. First, the Chinese government warned its citizens of the potential for massive failure and nationwide losses, yet they did not take enough precautionary legislative measures to prepare for the fallout. Today, thankfully, the Chinese government is working on combating peer-to-peer lending Ponzi schemes with increased regulations. Because these platforms are so new, the entire social lending industry was initially highly unregulated. Some analysts have ventured to guess that might explain how the Chinese government allowed so many companies to get away with robbery. Others assume the business model simply grew too fast, leaving rampant opportunities for corruption. Either way, the government is paying attention and fighting it now.

This type of spike and crash could happen anywhere. It's common for new industries to experience dramatic highs and lows in the early years. It takes time to prove battle readiness. If you choose to invest in peer-to-peer lending, know that it can be risky and that the projected returns might not be accurate. While many platforms claim that they can offer you something in the neighborhood of a 10% return, most of the time it is closer to 4-6% on average.

If you think you'd like to try out peer-to-peer lending, I'd advise you to look into multiple sites with different opportunities and invest a small amount on each one to find the platform that earns you the most passive income. Starting with a few hundred or even a thousand dollars on each platform will allow you to experiment with your methods, investigate different loan requests, and find what's best for your purposes. Next, I'll get into specific strategies for making peer-to-peer lending work for you.

How Peer-to-Peer Lending Works

P2P lending sites function just like many of the other online marketplaces you're probably familiar with. One of the original online peer-to-peer marketplaces is eBay. Today, over 1 billion listings are active on the site at any given time, and more than 2 billion transactions are made every single day. Amazon was founded in the same year, 1995, and has grown to be the world's largest retailer. Airbnb didn't come onto the scene until 2008, but it's already completely changed the face of vacation rentals. Uber didn't get started until 2009, but they have already demolished the stronghold of taxi drivers in America and launched an entirely new global industry known as "ride-sharing."

What these fast-growing and game-changing companies all have in common is that they are all online marketplaces. They provide a platform that connects buyers and sellers, and they make money by taking a cut on every transaction. Additionally, these platforms introduce an element of trust and transparency to the buying and selling process because every merchant on the marketplace gets rated and reviewed by everyone they do business with.

Peer-to-peer lending platforms work in the same way. First, an investor picks a platform, opens an account, and deposits money—which will be used to finance peer-to-peer loans. The nice thing about these platforms is they connect borrowers directly to investors, so shopping around for the right deal is incredibly straightforward. The site automatically determines the interest rates, timelines, and additional terms, plus they manage all of the transactions between borrower and lender. You don't have to worry about drafting up legal paperwork or hiring an underwriter. That's all taken care of.

Generally, since you don't interact with the borrowers and you may spread your investments around to hundreds of different loans at any one time, it doesn't make sense to write reviews for everyone you loan money to in the same way you would on Uber or Airbnb. Also, the general idea of these loans is to help people get back on their feet after a financial hardship, so you usually hope the same person won't be coming back to the platform for more. However, it is possible to assess the level of risk for each loan. The platform will provide you with a rating calculated using an algorithm that accounts for the borrower's credit score, monthly income, employment history, and other factors.

When you look around the marketplace for a potential loan applicant, you can check out the borrower's financial profile, the size of their request, what purposes your money will be used for, and other pertinent account details. This will help you gauge whether you want to do business with this particular person and how much money you'd like to loan out. Higher-risk loans are rewarded with higher interest rates, which can be a great deal for you but can also be hard for the borrower to repay. After you make an offer on a loan, the applicant will review your offer along with any others he or she received and will make a final decision on who to borrow from. Not all borrowers opt to take their full request from a single investor. Some choose to divide up their loan by taking multiple, smaller offers from many investors to reach the sum they seek.

Reliability is the main question most investors have about peer-to-peer lending. Will your payments come on time? What happens if your borrower runs out of money and can't make a payment? How often will the borrower default entirely on the loan? It's true that some loans default. And, unfortunately, when this happens there isn't much you can do to make up your losses. The platform will manage all of the weekly or monthly payments for you automatically, but it does not insure you in case of default. For this reason, it's up to you as the investor to keep a close eye on your loans and avoid high-risk scenarios.

Before you invest a lot of money in a particular platform, you should research its default rates, which varies from platform to platform. Also, unless you make thousands of loans, your actual default rate could vary significantly from the one advertised by the platform.

For instance, imagine you made 100 loans for $100 each on a marketplace with an average default rate of 3%. Your initial investment would be $10,000. Assuming an interest rate of 8%, you would earn $800 on this investment. Not too shabby! And you might get lucky and have zero of your borrowers default. How fortunate! You get to keep all $800. However, you could just as easily get unlucky and have 10 of your borrowers default on their loans. Ouch! Now you've made $800 but lost $1,000 of your principal. Overall, you've lost a total of $200. Theoretically, the more loans you make, the closer you'll come to the advertised default rate of 3%. However, it could take years to get there. Remember, it's a general average, not a steadfast rule.

Like crowdfunding, peer-to-peer lending is a crapshoot (yes, that's the technical term now). With this type of investment, you have no real way of vetting potential borrowers better than other lenders to gain a competitive advantage. You base your choices on the borrower's profile and the platform's estimate of risk. That's it. It's a numbers game. And for this reason, if you decide to try out peer-to-peer lending, I highly recommend diversifying your investments by spreading your money across multiple platforms and making multiple loans across each platform rather than one large loan. If this sounds like a lot of work, that's because it is. But it's necessary in order to reduce the risk of losing all your money.

As I mentioned, the interest rates are much better for riskier applicants, creating a huge range in peer lending opportunities. The rates for borrowers with good credit can be low and won't earn you much passive income. In some cases, you're actually better off investing in a CD, government bond, or money market account. As a reminder, the return rate on those are lower, and sometimes virtually zero, but with nearly complete security.

Another option is to allow the platform to automate loan approval for you. This is a bit of a mixed bag. The benefit of automated approval is that it reduces your time commitment to zero. You can just set it and forget it. However, the downside is that the site might approve lower rates or higher-risk loans than you desire. Additionally, the automated process removes negotiation. When you make offers manually, you can haggle with the borrower to come up with more agreeable terms, whereas setting your account to automatically reinvest your earnings can lead to overall worse deals and no opportunity to bargain.

A crucial piece of the online lending puzzle is that the predicted rate of return is not guaranteed by the platform. In most cases, the lending platform will quote you an 'expected' or 'target' return, but it isn't etched in stone. You can always earn less than your projection if the loan defaults, or if the borrower repays you at a faster rate than was initially agreed upon. When you're deciding to offer a loan, keep in mind that your projected rate is a best-case scenario.

Moreover, your investment doesn't earn you any money at all if it's not actively being loaned out. If it takes a week for your offer to be accepted, that's a whole week when you aren't making any passive income, so your cash is not working for you. It's nearly impossible to avoid this type of downtime.

Another way you can make less money than anticipated with peer-to-peer lending comes down to fees. Sometimes these aren't explicitly stated, so you have to do your own digging to find out how much a platform is going to charge you for their services. That can take hours, but it is a necessary part of your due diligence. Every platform has different terms when it comes to fees. Some sites only charge the borrower, where others change the lender. Others charge late fees, loan origination fees, and bounced-payment fees as well.

And don't forget the timeline and liquidity of your assets when planning out your peer-to-peer lending strategy. In general, many borrowers request a three- to five-year loan, which is a promising source of cash flow, but seriously reduces liquidity. When you factor in fees, early payments, and the potential for default, the overall return of your investments can be much lower than expected, which doesn't pair well with the risk you're taking on a three to five-year lock-up. It becomes difficult to justify a potentially 5% return on a risky, long term investment. This is why it's important to experiment with many platforms and borrowers to find a recipe that can earn you a decent return while minimizing risk.

Nonetheless, a well-balanced portfolio can earn you above-market returns—if you do it right. Next, I'll cover how to know when it's a good time to divert funds into a peer-to-peer platform.

Getting Started In Peer-to-Peer Lending

To know if peer-to-peer lending is the right passive income strategy for you, there are a few factors to consider. First, the amount of capital you have available to invest is paramount. Remember that your money is going to be tied up for three to five years. Plus, to make decent returns you'll need to continually reinvest your earnings. Peer-to-peer lending is a long-term strategy.

How much capital are you ready to put away for an extended period of time without being able to touch it? If your answer is $5,000 to $25,000, you might potentially be a candidate for this investing strategy. With less than $5,000 available you won't be able to diversify your capital across enough separate loans to mitigate the risk of default. And with more than $25,000 you could get involved in other passive income alternatives that are safer, less work, and offer higher returns and a larger upside. For this reason, $5,000 to $25,000 is the sweet spot for peer-to-peer lending.

With most lending platforms, you can break your investments down into "notes" that are as small as $25. As soon as these notes are repaid, they can easily be reinvested for more profit. As an example, you can spread a $5,000 investment across 200 notes at $25 each.

Just because you have $10,000 ready to go, doesn't mean you should invest it all in peer-to-peer platforms. It's no secret that peer-to-peer lending comes with significant risks and should be used primarily as a way to balance your investment portfolio. This is not going to be your main passive-income breadwinner. Many lending platforms openly acknowledge this potential investing mistake and recommend users only invest a certain percentage of their net worth on the site.

Another factor to consider is how much time you want to spend reviewing loan applications, sending offers, and negotiating with potential borrowers. To get decent returns with peer-to-peer lending, you'll need to do all of this manually, and that can easily add up to hours of work each week. That doesn't exactly put the "passive" in passive income. Of course, you can always go for automated re-investing if you don't mind sacrificing some returns. But what investor wants to sacrifice returns?

An important factor to consider is the economy. One great time to invest in peer-to-peer lending might be during a recession. As Jonathan Swift noticed, more people tend to turn away from bank loans and seek out social lending during times of economic downturn when the weaknesses of the centralized banking system are salient. Even as recently as during the recession in 2008, most peer-to-peer investors made money despite the stock market tanking.

However, in my opinion, the absolute best reason to get involved with peer-to-peer lending is if you want to finance a struggling small business or help out a family in need. Peer-to-peer lending is also referred to as social lending for good reason. When you loan money to your neighbors you have the power to help out others in your community. If you are a socially conscious investor and sleep better at night having put your money towards a good cause, private lending can be your new melatonin—that is, you can rest easy in your moral righteousness.

Report Card: Peer-to-Peer Lending

Time Commitment: Low

Getting started with peer-to-peer lending is as easy as creating a profile, linking your bank account, submitting funds, reviewing a few applications, and sending your first offer. You can get your investment up and running in a matter of a few minutes. This is one of the least time-consuming passive income vehicles on the market today, on par with the simplicity of purchasing shares in an index fund or mutual fund. If you use a fully automated strategy it will take no time at all. However, in order to maximize your returns, you'll want to spend a few hours each week vetting borrowers, negotiating loan terms, and reinvesting your earnings in a new set of loans.

Dealflow: High

There wouldn't be so many new peer-to-peer lending platforms coming out of the blue every year if there wasn't a lot of demand. Many people are clamoring for alternatives to traditional bank loans, student loans, and lines of credit. For this reason, there will always be high deal flow in peer-to-peer lending. The caveat is that high deal flow does not necessarily mean high quality. Many of the applications you receive will be highly risky, while others will be extremely safe but offer below-market interest rates. Finding the right balance takes significant effort.

Capital Commitment: Low

Since peer-to-peer lending notes can be purchased for as low at $25, you can get started with this investment class for less money than you might spend on a meal for two at TGI Friday's. Like crowdfunding, the minimums are astronomically low compared to traditional passive income investing strategies. No matter how low your bank account balance is, you almost certainly have the cash to start investing in peer-to-peer lending.

Knowledge Requirement: Low

The platform does most of the work for you. It assesses the risk level, provides an estimated return, and manages all transactions. Your knowledge requirement, therefore, is minor. You don't need to spend weeks researching the best deals, you just need to understand the numbers and information provided to you by the lending platform. It's basic, but again, to maximize returns, you may want to put in a few hours a week on it.

Return Potential (ROI): Moderate

The return potential is difficult to gauge. When you sign up, you'll be quoted a projected return of "up to 10%." However, you would only realize this in a best-case scenario. In the real world, defaults and early payments can steadily reduce that until you realize you are actually making be-low-market returns. Loans categorized as high-risk can boast return rates of up to 30%. However, the reason for these high rates is that borrowers in this bracket are more likely to default. In that case, you'll lose all your money. In truth, the overall average interest rate from peer-to-peer lending might be closer to 5%.

Risk Level: Moderate

The level of risk you take on with peer-to-peer lending is completely up to you as the investor. You can shop around, view borrowers' profiles, and make choices between high-risk and low-risk options. If you want to earn above-market returns, you'll probably have to make some risky offers. However, if minimizing risk is your main priority it's possible to select only borrowers with a low probability of default. The power is in your hands.

Upside: Low

There isn't any upside in peer-to-peer lending. The best-case scenario is that your borrower makes all of their payments on time and you end up recovering all of your principal plus a small amount of interest. There is no way you can ever end up with more money than the platform estimates you will make. If your borrower uses your loan to grow their business and is able to turn a great profit from your seed money, they will see the upside, not you.

The Bottom Line

Peer-to-peer lending is new and easy to use. It's popping up all over the world and shows resistance against economic downturns. It's growing so fast that not every government has figured out how to regulate it, which is why disasters are possible, as in the case of widespread fraud in China. Nonetheless, it is so simple and undemanding that anyone can get involved and start earning passive income rapidly. The rates can be great if you're willing to take on riskier loans. But the high rate of default on these usually eats up all your profits. If you don't have the resources to get started in safer and more lucrative passive income strategies, peer lending is one way to go. Diversifying across platforms and borrowers is one of the keys to making this passive income strategy work for you.

Don't like the idea of taking on risk? Peer-to-peer lending probably isn't for you. The passive income vehicle I'm covering next, annuities, may be more your style. With annuities you'll have guaranteed income for life. However, there are some drawbacks to consider, as you'll see when we meet up with actor Clint Eastwood.

Video Assignment #10: Cash Flow, not Net Worth

Although peer-to-peer lending may not be ideal if you're unwilling to take on higher risk, there is a huge benefit to sustaining a passive income cash flow. If your wealth is based on cash flow, it will survive long after you're gone. Conversely, a fortune based on net worth will soon disappear. Your goal should be to become a cash flow millionaire, not a net worth millionaire. In this video, we'll explain why.

To access the video, go to passiveincomethebook.com/10.

CHAPTER 11

Annuities

When I think of annuities, I like to imagine the scene from the film *Dirty Harry*, where Clint Eastwood delivers one of the most iconic lines of all time: "You've gotta ask yourself a question," Eastwood says, pointing the barrel of a .44 Magnum right between the eyes of his foe, "Do you feel lucky? Well, do ya, punk?" Neither man is certain whether Eastwood has a bullet left in his gun or not. Ultimately, the criminal gives in and allows himself to be captured. Gambling with his life, he decides, isn't worth it.

Annuities might not involve the risk of potentially having your brains blown out by hardscrabble gunslinger Dirty Harry Callahan, but this class of passive income-producing assets does involve gambling with your life. When you purchase an annuity, you are essentially placing a wager on how long you'll live. If you beat the odds, you come out on top. Otherwise, you might end up throwing away a lot of money.

This income model has existed for thousands of years, at least since Roman times. Many citizens in Ancient Rome, particularly soldiers, were paid a yearly sum for the remainder of their life—however long that may be. This may sound like a great deal for those on the receiving end. However, it actually appears to have been quite a sound strategy for the state of Rome compared to doling out a lump sum upfront. The republic realized that not every soldier would make it home. Therefore, some of the troops would not have to be paid at all, sparing the state an enormous expense.

In fact, one of the prominent Roman jurors responsible for popularizing annuities—or "annua," from the Latin word for yearly—is the same man who first designed the life expectancy table. Juror Domitius Ulpianus clearly understood the financial benefits and risks involved in paying someone annually for life. He even went so far as to create a detailed table that allowed the holder to estimate the projected lifespan of any Roman citizen based on years of aggregated census and mortality data.

The possibility of earning yearly payments for life came into prominence during the Dark Ages. This was a period when the mortality rate was incredibly steep. Historians estimate that up to one-third of all children born during this era did not survive to the age of 5, while adults who lived past 50 were considered old. War, famine, poverty, and plague were commonplace. Out of this morbid milieu, a new economic model was born based on annuities and the gamble to outlive the neighbors.

The ancient annuity, called a tontine, became a popular method of financing armies and wars during this period. Here's how it worked. A community of individual investors would cosign a tontine and contribute their initial investments into a central fund. Everyone alive at the end of the year would receive an equal portion of the remaining balance as a repayment on their initial investment. The more cosigners who died during each year, the larger the share would be for the recipients who remained alive. When you signed a tontine, you were essentially asking yourself "Do I feel lucky?" It was a system akin to a game of poker, in which the last man standing takes the pot. As long as you didn't pull the shortest straw and die first, your lot could be pretty profitable over time. And if not, well, you wouldn't be around to miss the money after your death anyways.

More than perhaps any other passive income vehicle, the annuity demonstrates clearly that life is money, and money is life. It's no coincidence that the word 'mortgage' originates from the French words for 'death' (mort) and 'pledge' (gage). You might not be surprised to hear that many annuities today are purchased from life insurance companies, an industry that is well accustomed to betting on the health—or lack thereof—of their policyholders.

In America today, annuities are not extremely popular, but are often employed by those seeking passive income during retirement. Annuity contracts come in a few different flavors, but typically they are between you (the "annuitant") and an insurance company. Unlike a tontine, modern annuities do not involve other investors. However, they do become more profitable the longer you survive. This is because your investment to an insurer is repaid incrementally every year for a fixed amount of time.

Unlike ancient annuities, you don't have to wait a whole year to receive a payment with the modern version. Payments can come monthly if you wish. In this way, you might contribute $100,000 to an insurer who agrees to repay you a fixed amount of $250 per month until you die. Therefore, after 50 years, you will have earned $150,000, or a 50% return on your initial investment. Now, $250 per month isn't much, but it's something, and it can add up if you live for a long time. Plus, it continues to pay out for as long as you live, with a complete guarantee and no fluctuation. It's incredibly safe, which is why it is a favorable method to generate retirement income.

Fixed annuities will only pay you a fixed and stable amount and there isn't any opportunity for upside. You can expect to receive the clearly defined interest payments as they are written in your contract, and nothing more. In this way, an annuity functions much like a CD. If your investment creates an upside for the insurance company, you won't see any of that extra income. You are stuck with the fixed rate. One big difference is that your money isn't liquid with an annuity, like it is with a CD.

Another type of annuity, called an indexed annuity, can offer you additional gains depending on the ups and downs of the stock market, similar to the way a money market account functions. Indexed annuities are invested into a market index like the S&P 500 and provide additional distributions on top of a guaranteed amount based on the performance of the index. However, because there are no downsides, the upsides are also capped. If your index leaps up to a 20% gain for some reason, you might only see a 4% increase on your end.

There is also a chance to invest your annuity into a mutual fund, an arrangement known as a variable annuity. In this case, you can build your own portfolio and invest your capital into funds of your choice. You don't have to be restricted to a specific market index. Like indexed annuities, this provides the opportunity to earn interest depending on the performance of your portfolio. However, the upsides are still capped at a maximum value regardless of how well the fund performs beyond the limit stated in your contract.

Annuities are differentiated into two main models based on how soon you will receive your first payment. The first option is an immediate annuity. With one of these you will start getting payments right away. The other option is a deferred annuity in which your funds will be held for a period of time before you start getting paid. In both cases, your taxes are deferred, so your money can compound tax-free until it is paid out to you or you make a withdrawal.

Because annuities are designed as long-term investment vehicles, you aren't supposed to take your money out until the maturation date. If it's a lifetime annuity, the idea is that you'll never withdraw your money. However, most annuities do allow investors to withdraw about 10% to 15% from their account in case of emergencies without incurring penalties. Beyond that, if you want to withdraw your money, you'll face steep fees.

Generally speaking, the overall returns from an annuity are minuscule due to high management fees and the fact that you're taxed on your disbursements even when they are deferred. To make a long story short, no one gets rich from annuities. If you end up living to a ripe old age after you start taking distributions, the total return on your annuity contract could be significantly higher than your initial investment, but it takes so long that it isn't going to significantly affect your lifestyle. And don't forget about inflation, which makes your annuity returns even less exciting.

Despite being safe, there is still some risk involved with annuities. If you die relatively soon, your annuity will wipe out your investment early and you might never see a full return. One of the best ways to mitigate the risk of loss due to a death is by opting to receive monthly payments for the rest of your life and including your spouse in your contract so he or she can continue to receive payments in the case of your passing.

At the end of the day, this passive investment vehicle works best not for the annuitant, but for the insurance company who issues it. If you die early or need to withdraw your cash for an emergency, you'll lose so much money it will completely wipe out any gains you made. Of course, if you're dead you might not care. Then again, if you'd like to build generational wealth, maybe you might. In any case, annuities must be used with extreme caution. We'll talk about how to tell if an annuity is right for you, next.

Broker Trying To Sell You An Annuity? Run!

In my world, annuity brokers are the equivalent of used car salesmen to the general public. Why is it that used car salesmen get such a bad rap? For one thing, they charge a relatively high price for a vehicle that loses half of its value as soon as you drive it off the lot. For another thing, they have been known to cover up problems and make a car seem better than it really is in order to make a sale. In my opinion, the big problem comes down to a misalignment of incentives. This same misalignment is at play when you purchase an annuity.

After you express interest in purchasing an annuity, your first step will be to speak with a broker whose job is to sell you something that isn't necessarily as valuable as they make it out to be. Brokers, like used car salesmen, take a substantial commission on selling you an annuity. In fact, annuities are among the most profitable financial instruments brokers are authorized to sell. The commission is usually 7% or higher, which is ridiculous for something that requires such little paperwork and only a few phone calls to seal the deal. Compare that with real estate agents who might make 6% on a house that takes months of hard work to list and sell.

The main market for annuities is people in their 60s and 70s who are looking for stable, predictable retirement income. For example, a broker might sell a recently retired couple on the idea of cashing in their $3.5 million 401k plan for annuities paying out a guaranteed fixed monthly income of $20,000 per month for the rest of their lives. To the couple, this may sound like a great deal. It's more than enough for them to live comfortably on for the rest of their days. However, it's really only a return of 6.8% on their money AND they don't have access to their principle any longer. When they die, **the insurer will keep their money**.

In reality, this is a fantastic deal for the broker who might have lined his pockets with somewhere in the neighborhood of $300,000 on this single sale, which he completed in the span of about three hours, leaving plenty of time to practice his putting in the afternoon. Additionally, it's a great deal for the issuing insurance company, who could turn around and re-invest that $3.5 million in a savvier instrument like a private equity fund or REIT and earn 8% interest plus an upside on the principal. That's how they can afford to pay such a high commission to the broker.

And I'm not just complaining because I think annuities are a bad passive investment vehicle compared to some of the other methods I've described. The truth is brokers are statistically proven to be less interested in what's best for you.

In 2016 the Department of Labor declared that brokers have to act as fiduciaries, meaning they have to put their clients' best interests ahead of their own. Later that same year the sales of fixed annuities dropped by 8% and sales of variable annuities dropped by a whopping 22%. There was no economic crisis to prompt such a drop, so analysts assume the decrease was a response from brokers who might have been worried about getting in trouble for selling annuities because they aren't in the buyer's best interest.

This could be a fluke. It's possible the drop was due to some outside factor, or a coincidence. Except, annuity sales dropped another 16% in 2017. That's on top of the 22% drop from 2016!

If this passive income vehicle still appeals to you, here's what you need to know to be successful. The main thing to keep in mind is how your life expectancy compares to the terms you are being offered. You want to be certain you'll turn a profit before you croak. On the short end, you can get a low-interest rate on an annuity that lasts about 4 to 5 years, or a longer, more rewarding rate on an annuity that will mature in 20 years or more. If you're 70 years old, how confident are you that you will get the full benefit of your annuity at age 90?

There's no argument that annuities aren't a safe investment. If you outlive the maturity date they are guaranteed to make you money. But I would argue they are the safest, riskiest investment because while you're guaranteed to make a profit, there's no guarantee you're going to be alive tomorrow. Your investment literally could be buried with you, especially if you opt for a longer-term annuity.

A possible strategy could be building an annuity ladder of staggered, short-term annuities. Perhaps each one matures in 5 years. This way, after 5 years, you'll start to see a profit every subsequent year, which you can reinvest so long as you live to see the ink dry. However, I think staggering CDs into a ladder is a better approach than annuities and is just as safe, with the added bonus of not leaving your family penniless should you kick the bucket ahead of schedule.

You'll also want to factor in which type of annuity is right for you. Is it immediate or deferred? Is it fixed or indexed? At the end of the day, the differences between these policies aren't huge, and some brokers will try to sell you on the idea that indexed, deferred annuities offer the best of both worlds, but that's not necessarily true. This might be an illusion of multiple-choice, where simply having options makes you think one must be preferable to the others. However, this is not necessarily the case. Remember, the upside is limited, and you'll still have fees and taxes on your withdrawals.

Another possibility is to put a massive one-time payment into an annuity, such as an inheritance, or lottery winnings, or a cash-out from the sale of your business. This way the money can be doled out to you over a specific time period. This works best if you aren't in the retirement planning phase of your life, meaning you are young, and your life expectancy is a bit more optimistic to reduce the risk that your inheritance or other large windfall will disappear entirely.

If you're in bad health, you might actually be in luck when it comes to annuities. Insurance companies will offer you a much higher interest rate on an annuity if you have a lower life expectancy. Does this sound manipulative? I think so. Insurance companies want to take your lump sum annuity payment and pray you don't live long enough to see it mature, so they tease you with a tantalizing rate. They might even tell you that if you die within a few months of purchasing the annuity, they'll pay your family a partial refund. But the damage is already done, most of the investment is unrecoverable, and the insurance company gains a huge upside. This all comes back to the central question I raise when it comes to annuities, how lucky do you feel?

Making an investment contingent on my survival is not a great feeling for me, personally. Unfortunately, many brokers of these annuities use fear-mongering tactics to make sales. They claim that greater monthly disbursements will help you pay for your increasing medical expenses. They might be right, but it's debatable whether you will actually see a net gain.

There's a saying in the business that goes along the lines of, "Annuities are not bought, they are sold." In my opinion, as an investor, you don't want to be the person being sold to. You want to be the one who does careful research and then takes advantage of a good opportunity.

Before you invest, you should also know that annuity interest rates aren't necessarily related to the federal funds rate. They might fluctuate a bit based on the treasury rates, but in general your interest rate is based on your own life expectancy, which is determined by age and sex. In this way, you might not get a lot of money as a young woman, but you can get a much better deal as an older man. Insurance companies know a lot about the mortality profiles of their clients, and they use this data heavily before quoting you for an annuity.

Lastly, not everyone needs an annuity. There seems to be a feeling among many Baby Boomers that annuities are a natural part of retirement planning. And, yes, annuities can definitely be helpful tools. But there are many roads to financial freedom out there. Don't be tricked into thinking that an annuity is right for you if it doesn't seem like a good fit. You can always invest in private REITs, corporate bonds, or dividend stocks to earn yourself regular, passive income with minimal risk. Next, I'll talk about when you might want to invest in an annuity, and when you might not.

How To Buy the Right Annuity

What most financial advisors recommend as the 'ideal' time to buy an annuity might shock you. With these passive income vehicles, you'll actually get a better deal the closer you are to death. Young people who are planning ahead and looking to get a jumpstart on creating a safety net for the future don't have the opportunity to greatly affect their lives with annuities.

Since annuities don't vary much in different economic climates, the time to buy is based on your own life expectancy rather than any measure of market confidence. Due to this, the 'recommended' best time to buy an annuity is around 70 to 75 years of age. If that is you, you might be in the prime demographic for the greatest annuity returns. At 70 or older, your life expectancy is relatively short, especially if you are male. Insurance companies are more than willing to take the chance that you will pass away before your annuity matures and leave your hard-earned principal to rest eternally in their coffers.

However, if you're in this age bracket and are in exceptionally good health, it might be reasonable to purchase an annuity for some easy and secure passive income. Manage to outlive your "life expectancy" and you could be rewarded handsomely, much like tontine investors of the Middle Ages, who pooled their money and distributed a portion every year to any-one who was still alive. On the flip side, if you're 40 and healthy and hoping to cash in on an easy, set-it-and-forget-it type revenue stream that can last you for the rest of your life, keep looking. The rate you're likely to receive won't be worth the hefty minimum required to buy an annuity. At this age, your $100,000 can be much more valuable when used to invest in other passive income vehicles, like real estate trusts and private equity funds.

But what if you're young and in poor health? Well, that actually might be a best-case scenario for annuities. Unhealthy individuals who have a chronic condition that conveys a shorter life expectancy can often get superior deals on annuities. And even if the unspeakable happens, your contract might continue to reap benefits through your spouse as a recipient. If you can manage some way to show that you are sick on paper, but you're confident you will actually survive for a long time, an annuity might be a worthwhile investment because you can laugh in the face of insurance companies (not to mention death, for now) who wager that you won't live long enough to cost them any money.

These 'enhanced' annuities for the unhealthy pay significantly more per annum than standard annuities, and in 2014, when new legislation allowed sickly people to access their pensions early, sales of retirement annuities to people of ill health plummeted by 44%. There may be an opportunity there.

Personally, if I were in poor health, I wouldn't want to purchase an annuity because they become better investments the longer you live. At the same time, it's difficult to find the best time to invest, as older people at greater risk of dying get better deals than younger people. Regardless of your age and situation, the odds are carefully calculated by the insurance company in order to stack the deck in their favor. For this reason, I'd only suggest purchasing an annuity if you have a shorter life expectancy but are in good health, and if you think you'll definitely outlive the maturity date of your purchase, with a spouse who can receive your investment should the worst happen.

Report Card: Annuities

Time Commitment: Low

When it comes to actually signing an annuity contract, the time commitment is incredibly low. There are many brokers selling annuities so it won't be hard to find a deal, and they earn great commissions so they will be highly motivated to follow up with you and get you locked in. The rates are consistent across providers, so shopping around to a bunch of different insurance companies is not necessarily recommended or worth it. The most time-consuming piece of the equation is waiting until you're at an age to take advantage of the best deals. But if you're already around 70 years old, you might be a prime candidate for an annuity.

Dealflow: Moderate

Because of the high commission structure associated with these, there's almost always going to be a long line of brokers and insurers ready to sell you an annuity. However, there are only a few main providers nationwide who underwrite the majority of annuities. And regardless of which provider you approach there are always going to be the same basic options available.

Capital Commitment: High

Most annuities are used as retirement tools, so this isn't the kind of investment you are going to make with $1000 in cash. They are designed to pay out a lot of money in order to keep you afloat after your working years. And they cost a lot upfront in order to make this possible. It's not unusual to pay $100,000 or $500,000 for an annuity, so it's no drop in the bucket.

Knowledge Requirement: Low

As the saying goes, "Annuities are sold, not bought." You don't need to know more than the bare minimum to get involved in an annuity contract. The knowledge you might need boils down to your own mortality risk and which type of annuity is best for you. By type, I'm referring to immediate versus deferred and indexed versus fixed. If you understand those two differences, you basically know everything you need to know before buying an annuity.

Return Potential (ROI): Low

If you're investing $150,000 to make $1,000 per month, you can see that the return potential isn't great. If you happen to live for 150 months so that your initial investment is returned, well, sky's the limit. If you live for 300 months you will have successfully doubled your investment. However,

25 years, a quarter of a century, is an awfully long time to wait to double your money.

Risk Level: Moderate

You already know what I have to say about risk. Do you feel lucky? Sure, the payments are highly secure, but you don't know if you'll live to see the investment mature. And if you don't, it's game over for your capital. It's not like taking a risk on a dividend stock or a commercial property, it's a risk on your health. This makes annuities starkly different from other investments when it comes to assessing risk. Your own death is harder to think about and predict than the stock market.

Upside: Low

There are virtually no upsides in fixed annuities. Indexed and mixed annuities can offer small upsides because your money will be invested into a mutual fund or stock index, but there's a huge tradeoff that can't be overlooked. While you are guaranteed not to lose money on your invest-ment, you also can't gain more than a determined upside, which might be 4% interest on top of your normal disbursement. If your investment returns 10%, you'll only see 4%. In this case, you would've been better off simply investing in a mutual fund in the first place.

On the other hand, if signing up for an annuity motivates you to quit your couch potato tendencies to "stick it" to the insurance man by living well past your expiration date, then you could say there is at least a silver lining to annuities.

The Bottom Line

Annuities are, quite simply, a bad deal. If you are in the right age demographic, between 70 to 75, you'll be able to get a good rate. However, you'll have to place a bet on how long you are going to live. Die before the annuity matures and the provider will keep your principal rather than passing it on to your heirs. If you're looking for a secure place to park your cash towards the end of your life, there are much better alternatives. For instance, create a family trust fund and use it to invest in real estate and dividend-paying stocks. With annuities, the interests are misaligned. The brokers and insurance companies who sell them to you don't actually want to see you make money—they literally prefer you *die*. Do yourself a favor and stick to assets where the person managing your capital only gets paid when you make money. Seek an alignment of interests.

In the next chapter, I'll cover the final passive income vehicle: angel investing. And we'll see how one investor made $53 billion on a single deal.

Video Assignment #11: Never Invest in Annuities

In this chapter's video, we'll cover a few more reasons why you should stay away from annuities. High fees, known as 'mortality and expense charges,' result in high operating costs for annuities. Expenses are up to three times higher than a typical mutual fund's expenses, sharply reducing your future investment returns.

To access the video, go to passiveincomethebook.com/11.

CHAPTER 12

Angel Investing

Angel investors are notorious for playing the long game: they invest in early-stage startups that are just getting off the ground, generally providing the first investor capital. At this point, a small investment of a million dollars or less can usually buy the angel investor a large stake of equity in the company. This means if the startup makes it big, the investor stands to see a significant upside. For instance, in August 2004, Peter Thiel made one of the most famous angel investments of all time, giving $500,000 to a young Harvard dropout named Mark Zuckerberg in exchange for a 10.2% stake in Facebook. He was the first outside investor to put money into Facebook and today Facebook is worth $537 billion, meaning Thiel's stake is valued at nearly $53.7 billion.

That's a return of over 100,000 times.

Of course, the reason Peter Thiel's investment is talked about by angel investors all over the world is because results like that are exceptionally rare. At the end of the day, every angel investor knows the majority of the companies they invest in won't go anywhere. Statistically, only one out of every ten startups reaches profitability. The odds aren't in your favor as an angel investor. However, when you do hit a winner, the returns can be massive.

Angel investing is thrilling, but before you get involved you have to be willing to lose everything. You'll also have to be willing (and able) to guide and advise the companies you invest in. They call it 'angel' investing because you'll act as something of a mentor for the startups you sponsor, regularly contributing advice, making important introductions, and voting on big decisions. This can be highly rewarding as well as exciting. And it offers you the opportunity to make a positive impact on the world through a product you believe in.

There are a multitude of recent platforms that allow accredited investors to find tech startups to invest in. Some of the more recognizable names are AngelList, FundersClub, and Alphaworks, which connect investors directly with companies. However, the best opportunities aren't listed on public sites where any investor can find them. The best deals are snapped up by experienced insiders long before they ever get to the point of posting on AngelList.

One of the themes with angel investing is that it requires a ton of work to master. You have to be knowledgeable and well-connected in the world of business and startups. Entrepreneurs don't only want your money; they also want your advice and Rolodex. If you don't have these things, you'll be at a serious disadvantage.

If you do choose a company that makes it big, they may start paying dividends to shareholders at some point. That's when the passive income starts rolling in. Until then, however, angel investing is a mountain of work without a molehill of return. You have to be prepared—financially and mentally—to lose your entire investment, because nine out of ten times you will.

And when you do land a promising deal with a fast-growing company, you must be prepared to be extremely hands-on for a long time. If you've started a company yourself in the past, you might know a thing or two about being a CEO, and this experience can help you reel in the big catch.

Having business acumen is invaluable for angel investing because it helps you tell the difference between the good teams with promising products, and the companies that are impending train wrecks with crippling internal failures. At the same time, you can help guide a growing business in a positive direction with your knowledge and experience. While there are always external factors a company can't control—like a worldwide health scare that dashes confidence, or a competitor that corners your market before you can debut your product—your hands-on managerial efforts can help improve your investment's chance at success.

Don't let the glowing success stories cloud your judgment. The media usually only covers the rare few startups that amass huge accolades, leading some investors to a biased outlook that angel investing is an easy ticket to making millions. Sure, it's possible, but it's not probable. Startups are constantly on the verge of failure and must be ready to pivot at any moment. The ones that do make it take years to finally get there, and the idea of an overnight success is, to put it bluntly, fictional.

Plus, a company that demonstrates rampant growth in a short period of time may be unprepared for rapid scaling and can end up collapsing. Sudden success can sometimes be catastrophic—when the 'hype' dies down, there better be a strong underlying product or asset that can keep the company afloat. The safest option for a company experiencing unfettered success might be the coveted "exit strategy," aka selling everything off to a larger company.

This is the goal of most angel investments, to eventually make a successful "exit." Once a company grows large enough to be acquired or to be traded publicly, the founders and early investors can kick back and enjoy massive upsides. At this point, they no longer have to run the company themselves. That becomes someone else's problem. Angel investors focus on getting the company off the ground, fast. Once a startup has broken through the atmosphere and is safely in orbit, you can take your hands off the controls and enjoy the ride.

Until the point of exit, however, your investments are illiquid and have a 90% chance of drying up. You might consider investing a small amount as an angel to hedge your bet, but the problem with that approach is later-stage investors will eclipse you, command control, and get an exponentially greater return than you if the company does take off successfully. The best way to go is to buy in for 10-20% of the company at a $3 to $5 million valuation. That will cost you $300,000 to $1 million, and you'll be taking a massive risk.

However, if your gamble pays off, the upside is unmatched.

So, how do you get started with your first angel investing deal? Well, it's a hell of a journey and requires a lot of leg work (plus a fair amount of luck), but I have a few tips that will help you better identify the safer options and expand your luck. I'll cover those next.

Do You Have What It Takes?

In order to make it big as an angel investor you have to be able to see a company's potential well before everyone else does. For instance, a little-known Japanese electronics company named Nintendo released a game called Donkey Kong in 1981 and it quickly became a hit. By the mid-'90s, Nintendo was one of the hottest brands on the planet, releasing games like Super Mario, Smash Bros, and Pokémon, along with gaming systems like the Super Nintendo, N64, Gameboy, and Wii. So, if you were an angel investor back in the '70s would you have been able to see the potential in Nintendo? Would you have made an investment?

Doubtful.

Actually, Donkey Kong didn't even come on the scene until nearly a century after the Nintendo Koppai company was first founded back in 1889. In its early days, Nintendo was known as a playing card company. They gained initial success manufacturing a card deck that was popular because it allowed people to play multiple gambling games with the same cards. In the 1950s Nintendo became the first company to print plastic playing cards, a major innovation. But international success still eluded the company, so they decided to move away from playing cards. Nintendo experimented with children's toys, vacuums, and a taxi service. They even had a brief stint managing short-stay love hotels...yes, those kinds of hotels. That idea went about as well as the vacuum one, which is to say, not particularly well.

In the 1970s Nintendo pivoted yet again, and this time they looked to electronics. They partnered with popular gaming company, Atari, and purchased other home video game consoles to be released under the Nintendo name. Then they started to develop their own consoles. Their electronics sold relatively well, but it was the release of the Nintendo Entertainment System (NES) in 1983 and the popular arcade game, Donkey Kong, that cemented Nintendo as one of the best home entertainment companies in the world. It wasn't long after this that Super Mario Brothers hit the shelves, and the rest is history.

The reason I bring up the story of Nintendo in a chapter about Angel Investing is because they are a perfect example of a company that went through years of trials, tribulations, and pivots before their ultimate rise to the top. In 1950 nobody could have predicted this obscure Japanese playing card company would become one of the leading video game brands.

That's how angel investing works. By the time it's obvious that a company is going to succeed, it's too late. You've already missed your shot. The time to invest is in the early days, before the company has figured out what its "thing" is yet. It's back when Nintendo was still making playing cards. Or running sex hotels. Often, a startup is going to be in rough condition when you decide to become an angel investor, but that doesn't mean they can't become the next Facebook.

Back when Twitter was called "Odeo," they were focused solely on connecting people with podcasts and growing communities of listeners. That was their business model. Then along came iTunes, which swallowed the podcast niche whole, leaving Odeo in the dust, scrambling for something to hold on to. What happened next was a revolutionary pivot: a status-updating, micro-blog service that is now used by teenagers and national presidents alike. You can even find "tweeting" in the dictionary.

Similarly, Andrew Mason created a crowdfunding site called The Point in 2007, which operated on a "tipping point" mechanism. If enough people contributed to a campaign, it would 'tip' and the project would receive funding. As a side project Mason started another platform, Groupon, which used a similar "tipping point" concept for local deals. If enough people pledged to do an activity, it would tip, and a special discount would be unlocked. Groupon quickly eclipsed The Point in popularity and became the daily deal tycoon we know today.

There are countless examples of startups that had to pivot to earn themselves a place on the world stage. As an angel investor you are not investing in the current product or even the current industry space that a company is occupying—you're investing in the team. You're betting on the founders.

Back when Uber was still in its beta phase, a software glitch prevented users (some of them potential investors) from paying with their credit cards at the end of the transaction. It's easy to see why many decided not to invest in the company after that experience. However, every investor who walked away after that early-stage bug is probably kicking themselves in the pants right now.

Focus on the team, not the current execution.

One great way to judge the team is to put yourself in your old shoes. You know, the ones you wore in your 20s when you were trying to figure out which company filled you with a sense of promise. Look for companies that you would have joined on the ground floor. Find companies that are working on a big problem or issue you care about. Consider companies that have a strong sense of integrity and seem likely to treat you as a trusted investor and angel with the proper respect. If they are not yet a success, see if you can spot the obvious flaws preventing it. These are all things to consider that will help you parse out the rotten eggs from the good ones when considering an angel investment.

Personality is just as valuable for identifying a solid team. You need to make sure the founders and early hires are passionate and committed, but won't let their hubris and excitement overshadow their business rationale. They need to be hard workers—as well as smart workers—who are unafraid to admit when they are wrong and willing to ask for help when they need it.

A solid team with an intelligent and personable founder is not enough to build an entire business around, nor is it the only factor determining if you should invest. A company also needs a working product or business model. It's true that the product might change over time, and glitches can be worked out, but the current delivery of product is the scaffolding upon which you build the rest of the company.

My next big piece of advice is to get involved with partners. Partners are seasoned veterans who have seen the market morph and transform a million different ways. It's impossible to predict all of the external market forces that will rain down on a business or industry, but the right partners can help you steer through any storm. They will have the experience to navigate poor conditions better than the startup's founders and employees.

When you do get involved, you need to scrutinize every detail of the deal. If you don't have the firsthand executive experience in a particular industry yourself, do the research and bring in business professionals who can honestly evaluate your company and the market. Restructure the management if you have to, because internal issues can be just as deadly as external ones when it comes to startup failure. Bring in more investors if that's what the company needs to reach the next stage. Invest in the tools to collect and analyze data so you can nip problems in the bud and adapt or pivot immediately. Realize that even perfect, no-brainer, 'sure-thing' businesses can fail. In fact, it happens every day. It's critical to be hands-on and not to ignore any issues. But despite all your efforts, the company is still not guaranteed to have a breakthrough.

When it comes to angel investing, I recommend you take the small portfolio approach. Since 90% of startups fail, you're playing a numbers game. Your first few investments are almost certain to go south. I think planning to invest in ten to fifteen companies is a good ballpark for what it will take to find a winner. At the same time, you don't want to put your whole financial portfolio into startup funding, because it's far too risky. A good metric to use is to invest a maximum of 10% of your overall liquid funds into an angel investment portfolio at any one time, and to be prepared to lose all ten percent. As you gain experience and have some successes, you can start to increase this number.

Finally, you have to know where to find high-quality deals—and it takes a lot of running around. Most of the time, successful angel investors leverage their network of colleagues to find opportunities. If you are close with the alumni network of your university, there may be some promising graduates who you have an 'in' with. Another pool of connections is the so-called angel investing "mafia," which is a group of early employees at a successful startup. These people usually develop a lot of high-quality connections with other companies on their way up. If you've started your own business or worked in a startup yourself, former coworkers could be a great place to start when researching high-quality opportunities.

If you venture too far beyond these types of close connections, you'll almost certainly become a bottom feeder. The deals you'll receive on a site like AngelList will mostly be the ones that other investors already passed on. I'm not writing them off altogether: there are definitely some sleepers that fly under the radar, but odds are you'll have a hard time finding one.

The Qualities Of A Good Angel Investor

With $74 million in funding from heavyweight investors like Mark Zuckerberg, plus fourteen million users across seven hundred universities, Handshake seems like a startup with a great chance of going big. The company is young, but the brand is already well established. Plus, it's in the hands of impressionable students and alumni who might one day adopt the platform as an alternative to LinkedIn. Nonetheless, it would be a surprise if this popular networking company managed to reach an initial public offering. Statistically, only 0.1% of startups ever make it to an IPO.

Look a little longer and the numbers are staggering: every year, tens of millions of people start a business and try to get it off the ground. Of those, about three million end up incorporating. Less than a million of those ever end up hiring an employee who is not a founder. Then, more than 50% of those fail or disappear completely. Another 20% of the remaining startups are acquired by a larger company. And only 0.1% ever go public, despite the immense effort and capital invested.

When you're asking yourself whether you should become an angel investor, there's a lot to consider. This decision definitely should not be taken lightly. First, you should only get into angel investing if you're ready to lose money. A lot of money. You'll be putting some of your capital into one of the riskiest types of assets available. Considering the high cost of angel investing and the low probability of success, you have to be prepared to lose your investment before you see any returns. Before you get into this field, you should already have the kind of well-balanced portfolio that allows you to stomach a substantial loss should the business go under.

It would be foolish to dump half your portfolio into a single startup. In fact, it's generally recommended to keep highly risky investments like angel investments to just 10% of your overall portfolio. Before you invest in a startup, you need to be an accredited investor with a lot of liquid capital at your disposal. You'll have to be comfortable investing at least $500,000 in multiple startups if you want to have any real shot at success. Therefore, a good place to start is to make investments in ten companies that all show enormous potential and have a stellar team. That would put you in the neighborhood of $5 million for your first round of angel investments. Keeping those contributions at or below 10% of your portfolio means you'll want to have an overall portfolio size of $50 million or more before you get serious about angel investing.

You also shouldn't get started as an angel unless you love getting companies off the ground and getting your hands dirty. In the startup world, an angel investor is expected to play a key role in the success of the business as a mentor. This means it's helpful to have some prior success in running a company before you get into angel investing. It's not necessary, but it will greatly improve your ability to be a successful angel. Angels aren't simply good investors; they are good leaders with strong executive backgrounds who put in a lot of work to drive the company towards success.

An underrated quality to be aware of before you decide to invest in startups is your personal and professional network. There are many angel investing platforms that can connect you with new ventures. However, personal relationships allow you to access more promising opportunities. When you have connections with founders you've worked with before or who are vetted by the other entrepreneurs in your circle, you might catch word of a new startup with a solid product and team before the founders turn to a public platform to look for funding. The early bird gets the worm. If you can swoop in fast and create a connection with the CEO, the company might never venture online for financial support. Indeed, many of the top startups in recent years never posted an ad on AngelList. They easily connected to savvy investors through their network.

Knowing other angels is another huge asset to help you get started and decide when to invest. Angels with experience can offer wisdom on what they consider a good opportunity and how to approach it. You might join an angel group to make connections and find more investors with whom to pool funds.

Last but not least, you'll know you're ready to invest when you've found the perfect company and you can be sure they have a solid team. The more research you do prior to investing, the more potential insights you can generate, which can be your most valuable tool in assessing a promising deal. If you have deep insight into a particular market, you'll be aware of things other investors might not realize and you'll be able to capitalize on the next big thing.

Report Card: Angel Investing

Time Commitment: High

Of the eleven passive income investment opportunities I've covered in this book, this might be the least passive of all. It requires a commitment to continually engage with the companies you invest in on a regular basis to provide ongoing support. Whether you restructure the company and get involved with management or simply act as a mentor, you have to be available and willing to step in to offer insight on big decisions and path-altering changes for the companies. Otherwise, you're not performing your due diligence or protecting your investment.

Dealflow: Low

While there are millions of startups all begging for funding, the deal flow for angel investing isn't great. For one, it's extremely expensive so you have to pick and choose your deals carefully, or else you'll run out of funding rapidly. And not every startup wants the mentorship of an angel. Moreover, most startups fail! Finding the right companies to invest in takes a tremendous amount of time and legwork. You'll have to go through your options extensively to find the shiny needle in the haystack.

Capital Commitment: High

If you make a small investment in a startup, it probably will not make a noticeable impact on their ability to succeed. In order to be truly impactful, you need to invest around half a million to a million dollars. If you can't invest this amount, other angels can, and their shares of the company will overtake yours, minimizing your returns if the company does indeed take off. It would be a shame to do all the work to get a company to the finish line without receiving a sizable share to walk away with.

Knowledge Requirement: High

It pays to know a thing or two about executive management. Most angel investors have master's degrees, and about half of them have an MBA in addition to prior experience and success in the business sector, specifically as founders or C-level employees. In this way, there is a strong correlation between knowledge and success as an angel investor. This isn't like investing in stocks and bonds, which will generally give you a return even if you know nothing about how the companies you're purchasing are run. Angel investors need to understand the ins and outs of a business (and often the industry) to lead a company to profitability.

Return Potential (ROI): Moderate

The returns are insanely good when you can get them, but banking on steady returns is a losing bet. Most companies will not generate enough money to pay you back for your investment, and if they do, it will take years. Startups generally want to reinvest all of their profits in growth rather than paying them out to shareholders as dividends. This means you aren't likely to see regular payments for many years.

Risk Level: High

What more can be said about a 99% rate of failure? Combine that with the high cost of getting started and you've got a risky combination. Most angel investors are well aware that they might lose it all. They usually get involved because they love to grow businesses and push entrepreneurs to success. If you're not passionate about startup culture and the challenge to break into a market, there isn't much else that can justify taking such a huge risk.

Upside: High

The unparalleled upsides are what draw many to angel investing. If you do strike gold and get in early with a company that makes it, your initial investment could multiply a hundredfold or more. Of course, as most things go, with the high reward comes the high-risk.

The Bottom Line

Angel investing is for the sophisticated investor who is ready to lose their entire investment for a chance at the big time. It's not safe, it's not easy, and it's not quick. It's a long, expensive process that will likely end in failure. However, it is one of the most exciting investments you can make. It's thrilling to help a company start generating serious money, taking on new employees, and reaching a wider audience. It's rewarding to take a startup all the way to the world stage, or even just to the local market. If you do succeed, you'll be the envy of all your friends because you did the impossible and made a ton of money doing it. And once a company matures and starts returning profits to shareholders, you'll have a massive amount of cash flow on your hands.

With these eleven options for generating passive income now fully explained, I'll cover my best tips for getting your own portfolio started. Plus, the four different investor types and how to determine which type you are.

Video Assignment #12: Strategies of the Ultra-Wealthy

In our final video, we'll take a look at some strategies of the people that are the most likely to be angel investors: the ultra-wealthy. Wealth preservation among the ultra-wealthy is different than it is among regular investors. For the ultra-wealthy, preserving wealth means maintaining a certain income level and lifestyle for their children and grandchildren.

To access the video, go to passiveincomethebook.com/12.

CHAPTER 13

Getting Started

The "right" investment for anyone depends on many different factors including risk tolerance, knowledge, and the amount of capital you have available to invest. At the end of the day, only you can know what's truly best. However, I can certainly provide some guidance. After spending decades in the finance industry and working personally with hundreds of different investors to find the perfect balance of passive income assets for their portfolios, I've learned what to consider and how to make the right decisions about where to put your money. This chapter will explain my approach. There is also another chapter that goes even more in depth about exactly how to apply the ideas in this book to your own investing portfolio, which you can read by visiting passiveincomethebook.com.

In my experience, there are four general 'types' of investors out there. Each of these people approaches investments differently. Some are risk-takers, while others study investments for months before making a move. Some adopt a global perspective while others stick to local investments that they have personal experience with. See which style resonates for you and then check out my recommendations for the types of assets you might want to consider.

I call these four styles: the Maverick, the Salary Replacer, the Crate

Digger, and the Global Opportunist.

The Maverick

This type of investor is ready to roll the dice and hope for a massive payoff. They are often drawn to risky lending opportunities, private fund investments, volatile stocks, and angel investing. For the Maverick, it all comes down to growth. They want to put their money into something with the potential to go big, and they are willing to accept a high level of risk in order to find it. Maverick investing is extremely exciting and feels high-speed, but it actually requires a large degree of patience as well as a willingness to endure plenty of setbacks and failures. These investors know it might be years before their investment takes off—or it might never happen.

These investors are the early adopters in your life. They were taking Uber, eating sushi burritos, and renting their apartments out on Airbnb before you'd even heard of these things. When flying taxis hit the market, the Mavericks will be the first ones in line at the helipad.

If the possibility of helping entrepreneurs break conventions and change the world sounds exciting, you might be a Maverick. These are the dreamers who believe a revolutionary idea can overtake an entire industry and transform the way people live their lives. If you're willing to take a big risk, invest a decent amount of capital, and want to go 'left' when everyone else seems to go 'right,' then you're the type of investor who might be able to earn the largest kind of returns available. Thinking outside of the box is your secret weapon. Of course, you're also the type of investor who might lose everything chasing the "big one."

If you identify with this approach, then you'll need to have the time and capital available to invest in a VC fund, make a handful of angel investments, or give out some private business loans. You should be ready to lose a lot of money on failed startups. You aren't the type who will be satisfied with a safe, low-interest certificate of deposit. Instead, you'll want to spread your portfolio out across a variety of riskier investments so you can hang on to the few that might go big.

To be a good maverick, you must also be ready for your investment to change direction at any moment. Many startups and private funds alter their asset allocation strategy a few times before they settle on something that sticks, so you'll have to be flexible and willing to see your money disappear. You also need to have faith in the teams you invest in, not just the specific products. Startup success often comes from pivoting to something new. Mavericks are often full-time investors with extensive experience in whatever sector they choose to invest in.

At the end of the day, being a Maverick is thrilling but risky, so spread out your investments and be prepared for anything.

The Salary Replacer

The Salary Replacer isn't looking for rapid, risky gains that might evaporate overnight. This type of investor just wants to build up enough passive income to replace their entire salary so they can retire early. At the same time, their main concern is to not lose money. They value stable growth and safe profitability.

These investors usually haven't made millions at the helm of a startup or created an empire based on flipping houses. More likely, they are regular people with good jobs who are smart about saving their money and making safe investments. One day they will replace their salary with passive income and retire to a life of relaxation and adventure, but they aren't trying to get there at a breakneck pace. They usually opt for plain-vanilla, safe, low-risk investments with low fees, like bonds, index funds, and mutual funds. As their fortune grows, these types of investors will start to make larger investments in REITs and private equity funds where they can obtain high returns and attractive upsides without having to spend time managing their investments. Because most of them work full-time, they don't want anything that's going to take up their limited free time.

If you are this type of investor, you are just like most of the people who invest in my funds at Four Peaks Partners. You'll want a trustworthy team to take care of the details for you so you can just sit back and collect the checks. After a few years, you'll be making more from your investments than you do from your full-time job. For Salary Replacers, that day is often highly emotional. It's when you finally become completely free to live your life however you want.

The Crate Digger

This name comes from the old school hip-hop DJ's who would rummage through the cheapest, bottom-shelf crates at the record store, searching for buried treasure and deep cuts. It's tireless work, flipping through stacks and stacks of pressed vinyl for the next hot sample, but it's worth it when you drop a track that makes the audience lose their minds. Crate Diggers will search obsessively for overlooked assets that are selling for strangely low prices. This is time-consuming, with long droughts in between return rainstorms, but these investors are obsessed with quality and willing to sift through hundreds of opportunities until they find a Billboard chart-topping hit.

The Crate Digger is also a perfectionist. They prefer hard data, promising Form 10-Ks, and solid management. But they also aren't afraid to stray from the norm, looking under rocks to find the diamond in the rough. Their portfolio might be focused on desirable real estate assets in developing neighborhoods, or micro-cap stocks with great numbers, rather than the S&P 500.

Like Mavericks, these investors are looking for innovation, but instead of taking a handful of big risks to find the one or two companies that will change the status quo, Crate Diggers are patiently awaiting the highest quality opportunities possible. The assets they invest in can be just as bold and demanding as Mavericks, but they are significantly less risky.

The Global Opportunist

This investor always keeps an eye on international opportunities and stays informed on the differences between various economies and currencies around the world. Their investments follow the markets with the best growth opportunities.

These investors do not base all of their tactics purely on statistics. They study intangible variables as well, like international politics, and often get involved in newer, unregulated industries so they can ride the wave. A global opportunist tries to get ahead of the trends. There's a lot of risk and innovation involved, but investing in growing economies allows for a lower entry barrier.

At the same time, these investors must be up to date on news and popular trends, track changes to relevant international laws, and expect a lack of transparency from foreign companies.

If you're interested in this investment style, you might look into international REITs, which can allow you to target real estate in growing economies. Also, active foreign real estate investing, angel investing, and private funds might also be good fits for Global Opportunists.

Due Diligence for Passive Investments

In November 2012, $8.8 billion accidentally slipped through the cracks of technology giant Hewlett-Packard. The company had been going through a rough patch with a high level of employee turnover, a constantly changing leadership, and a series of lackluster fiscal quarters. They needed to alter their approach. Selling hardware wasn't paying the bills anymore, and software looked like it might be the gold ticket to renewed profitability.

So, HP turned to a tried-and-true strategy of flailing mega-corporations the world over: acquire a hot new startup. They decided to buy British software company Autonomy for $10 billion.

Even though the deal was reviewed by over 300 people within HP, there was a small oversight no one picked up on. Autonomy had been "artificially inflating" its records. Their accounts were exaggerated—and not subtly. In fact, there were numerous blatant errors that HP's army of auditors some-how failed to recognize. Their lack of thorough due diligence in reviewing Autonomy's claims led to a minor write down of $8.8 billion...and a whole lot of finger pointing.

In some ways HP was the victim in this story. After all, they weren't the ones to fudged the numbers. They were swindled! Autonomy took advantage of them, right? Actually, HP's problem was a lack of diligence. They shot themselves in the foot by failing to look closely at what they were buying before they signed on the dotted line. Their mishandling of the bogus deal led to a series of lengthy litigations and investigations from the SEC, FBI, and the United Kingdom's Serious Fraud Office. Shareholders' portfolios tanked as a result, lawsuits chastised HP for its neglectfulness, and the technology behemoth's recently appointed CEO, Léo Apotheker, was fired. In 2015, HP ultimately agreed to pay $100 million to investors who had purchased HP shares between the acquisition of Autonomy in August 2011 and the $8.8 billion write down in November 2012.

The infuriating thing about this type of financial disaster is that it was entirely avoidable. HP didn't need to lose billions on the Autonomy deal. All they had to do was take a closer look at the company's financials before agreeing to the $10 billion price. Write this down: due diligence is worth billions.

Before you decide to invest in anything, it's important to do your homework. You'll need to dive deep into the financials of every possible investment. This means evaluating the market, performing a risk versus reward calculation, and taking the time to fully understand the ins and outs of a deal. You don't want to get caught taking phony data like HP, so double-check everything. And if you don't know how to evaluate a deal, it might be best to hire someone familiar with the industry to help you estimate hidden costs.

Often you will have to spend additional capital to keep your investment on track after your initial payment. For example, if you're investing in a startup, you might need to loan more seed money than expected before the company can start turning a profit. Be prepared for multiple rounds of financing. If you're investing in real estate, you need to factor in taxes, closing costs, rehab costs, and vacancy costs, as these hidden expenses can significantly cut into your profits. It's beneficial to consider how expensive your investment might be from every angle and assume the worst and be surprised by the best.

Going over the personnel for every deal is just as important as analyzing the numbers. If you aren't yet knowledgeable about an industry niche, find an expert to help you build a team. Bringing in financial advisors gives you a significant advantage also—you cannot prepare for things you don't know about. Plus, no matter how much research you conduct on your own, it's unwise to take a risk on an investment for the first time without consulting someone who has experience. The professionals with years of experience in a niche will always know something you don't.

It's also very helpful to consult with a lawyer who specializes in whatever type of asset you're investing in. Every industry and every state have specialized rules and regulations that you must learn to follow as part of your due diligence. You don't want to get caught running into unanticipated legal roadblocks after you invest because you didn't do enough homework in the first place. It's invaluable to hire an experienced lawyer who can help you navigate every new investment, especially if you are drafting contracts or negotiating an agreement.

It's also often the case that you will need to hire some people to execute various aspects of a deal. For instance, you'll need contractors for rehab and property managers to oversee your housing investments. Expenses, mistakes, and delays can pile up and cut sharply into your bottom line with these types of hires. You must vet these people personally and supervise them closely. In many ways, they will be responsible for your investment. If you get ripped off by someone you hired, it's your own fault.

You also might want to consider what types of insurance are needed for any investment you get involved with. This is something most amateurs overlook, and it can be a costly mistake. For instance, if one of your contractors gets injured while rehabbing your property you could be liable for medical expenses and disability costs. If a company you invest in ends up causing pollution that needs to be cleaned up for $2.8 million, you could be asked to fork over some cash. If the apartment building you just purchased burns to the ground, your passive income stream also goes up in smoke... unless you are properly insured. It's always a good idea to be over-insured. These types of policies are generally inexpensive and worth the money. Find a good insurance agent who can help you get coverage for all of your deals.

If you're considering investing in a company, it's important to look not just at the product idea and sales projections, but also at how the company represents itself. It might seem like "soft" research, but due diligence includes spending time reading through the company's mission statement and values. Consider whether they really live up to the ideals they claim to stand for. Does it seem like their business practices are in line with their proposed goals and guiding principles? You're looking for a company that can not only hit their sales targets, but do it in a way that's in line with their core values and won't be cause for a negative media storm should things go awry.

Due diligence has no boundaries. Every piece of information can add value to your investment decision, so don't discount anything you come across. The more thoroughly you can evaluate the quality of an investment and the costs that might be involved in the future, the better you'll be able to judge how much the deal is actually worth so you can maximize profitability.

This is especially important for passive income investments because the whole point of these assets is to generate regular income without requiring much supervision or active work. If you can't walk away from the operations of your passive investment without feeling confident that your money will continue to work for you in your absence, you haven't done enough research. However, this isn't to say that you should ignore your investments. Due diligence is ongoing. It isn't something you do once and then forget about. It also means managing your portfolio by checking in on your investments on a regular basis to make sure they are performing as anticipated. This way if anything unexpected comes up you can act quickly to ensure your passive income is secure.

Sounds like a lot of work, right? Yes, exactly! All good things take time. It can take months or years to perform due diligence for a passive income investment, especially when you're hunting for massive real estate deals or angel investments. The bigger and more complex a deal gets, the more due diligence is required.

Even if you hire a reputable firm like mine, Four Peaks Partners, to manage your investments, you should still perform due diligence. I've been doing this for decades, but I still recommend every potential client does their own research to ensure my firm is the right fit for their needs. Email my team, team@fourpeakspartners.com, to inquire about our history. Ask high-profile partners about their experiences with our firm. Get the honest truth. I'm not trying to convince you that I'm a good choice. I'm asking you to put Four Peaks to the test so you feel confident that putting your money into one of our funds the best move you can make for your financial future.

But you won't know until you do your research. That's what it all boils down to.

Don't choose an investment simply because it sounds good or because your friend said it was a good deal. You need to know exactly what you're investing in before you put your hard-earned money into anything. Check the financial history, learn about the market, choose your team, calculate risk and reward, and investigate the seller. If you want to generate passive income for yourself, you'll need to get serious about vetting deals carefully.

The Ticket to True Financial Freedom

Your job doesn't have to be a dead-end for you to feel stuck. In fact, you can be on top of the world and still feel chained to a desk. When I was an agent at William Morris, I had what most people would consider a "dream job." I was in the top 1% of wage earners, interacted with celebrities on a daily basis, and had ridiculous perks like a company car and free tickets to every event I wanted. But all that glitters isn't gold—especially in Hollywood.

What I truly craved was freedom. I wanted to live life on my own terms and chart my own course. I wanted to find a way to keep earning the same high salary but without feeling suffocated. So, I started making passive income investments. First, I took an honest look at my current position to decide what kind of investments made the most sense for me. I had plenty of capital and was ready to put in the time to learn a new industry and vet potential investments, but I didn't want to spend a lot of time managing my investments once I'd made them. This meant angel investing and private equity weren't a good fit. Also, I didn't have experience or connections in real estate, so private lending was off the table too. And crowdfunding didn't even exist yet. I settled on active real estate investing and hired a property manager to handle leasing and maintenance.

I studied every real estate book I could get my hands on and quickly started taking risks on cashflow-positive properties in Texas. It only took four years for my new passive income to match my agency salary, allowing me to quit my job.

The path to financial freedom looks different to everyone, but the basic milestones are the same. To understand your best route to independence and your dream lifestyle, you should start by assessing your current position. In my role as a fund manager, I see people every day from a variety of different backgrounds who hope to put their money to work. I've seen contractors save up $100,000 and snowball it into a vast fortune. I've helped lawyers supplement their salaries and pay for their kids' college tuition. I've even known farmers who made wise financial decisions and now bring in more from passive investments than from agriculture.

Many of these wealthy investors don't have top-percentile salaries. Most aren't looking to quit their jobs...at least, not yet. They love what they do, but they also love the feeling of freedom that comes from doing work purely for the joy and not the money.

Whether you aim to quit your job, build a retirement fund, or create a passive income machine that will support your family for generations, the strategies I've covered in this book can make your dreams a reality. Now it's time to choose a path and get started. It's OK not to have everything figured out quite yet, but it's important to begin somewhere. Maybe you'll start with buying CDs, working to save up a year's worth of income. Or maybe you'll jump right into real estate or dividend stocks. The critical thing is to begin.

I've made it as easy as possible by providing report cards for each investment class that will help you determine the best fit for you. Give it some thought and go for it. But don't give it so much thought that you delay action. Getting going is more important than getting it perfect. You'll inevitably learn as you go.

Start with an asset class you can afford and invest an amount that you can afford to lose. If you can only invest $1,000 or $10,000 comfortably, that's OK. You'll have more to play with soon enough. Start with the vehicle that is best suited to your current resources, and once you have a strong monthly influx of passive cash or have saved up, branch out to the pricier options.

When you understand your target asset and know how much you want to spend, open an investing account. This could be an IRA or 401k if you're preparing for retirement, or a taxable brokerage account if you plan on replacing your current salary with a passive income stream. Brokerage accounts have fewer restrictions, so it's easier to take your money out and you'll have more flexibility with your investments. When you decide how much to put into your passive investment account, be careful not to risk a majority of your net worth.

You don't need a massive amount of capital to open an account and get started. There are low minimums for these accounts, so you can get into the game at practically any time.

Building up passive income takes patience. It doesn't happen over-night. Consider how long you would be willing to wait before you start earning a return. Are you looking for quick turnarounds, within a year? If so, short term CDs and lending contracts might be good options. Interested in a more long-term strategy, such as acquiring businesses or properties that might not be profitable right away, but have a greater potential for future returns? If you don't need to see a profit immediately, I'd recommend starting with some stable long-term investments that can pay you for years to come. The more of these you stack up, the faster you'll be able to build a substantial, sustainable, generational revenue stream.

Picking a timeline for your investments is relatively easy, but assessing the level of risk you're willing to accept can be much more difficult. In this case, consulting with some trusted advisors and professionals can greatly improve your chances of earning a healthy buck. If you're new to an asset class, you might not be aware of all the possibilities for your investment to go awry. I'd recommend checking in with a professional who can help you clarify just how big of a gamble you're making. With their advice, you can accurately determine whether the risk versus reward ratio is worth it to you. Some investors prefer low risk with low interest while others are itching for a huge return. Before you decide how big of a risk you want to take, get an expert opinion to help you assess the investments you are considering.

To keep yourself on track, I always recommend setting a goal for how much total capital or monthly passive income you'd like to have. In my opinion, it's better to view your investment strategy as "How much money can I make per month, passively?" rather than, "What's my endgame account balance?" I'd take massive cash flow over huge liquid capital any day of the week.

It's also good practice to set a goal for how much you'd like to invest per month in your passive income investments. Then set up an automatic deposit from your checking account into your brokerage account every month for that amount. Even if a few hundred dollars a month is all you can afford, it's important to continually add capital to your passive income machine. As your salary increases, you can increase these monthly deposits. Once you begin to see steady cash flow from your investments, you can start to reinvest your earnings each month to further build your passive income.

Don't get too comfortable or you might become over-reliant on a single asset and put yourself at risk should the market unfavorably change. Once you gain knowledge and experience in your primary investment class, it's a good idea to choose a second type of asset to master. Then a third.

There's no better way to get started than to aim for mastery. Read some books, enroll in a course, and start studying until you feel confident enough to make an investment. The best thing I did was hit the books hard. The second best thing I did was find mentors who could advise me on my early deals. I learned so much from the wise counsel of these experienced investors. Get into networking groups in your area to meet other investors. Connect with people on LinkedIn. Send an email. If real estate is what you're interested in, you can get in touch with me. I'm on LinkedIn and love hearing from readers. I get a lot of messages, but be persistent (and polite) and I'll be happy to give you some tips or make some introductions.

Hopefully by now you've made up your mind, picked an asset class, and started saving money. Congratulations! What next? Monitor your investments carefully to see how they are performing and make adjustments as necessary. Stay on your toes in case you need to adapt and change. It might take a few years or a few approaches to find what works best for you but once you nail it, all that's left to do is sit back and watch the checks roll in.

Starting Your Own Passive Income Portfolio

Using the strategies I've shared in this book, I was able to replace my salary and quit my job—and now you can too. Once you achieve a steady flow of monthly passive income you can choose whether you want to work, or not. You can spend your time managing your investments, or hire someone to do it for you. You can decide to travel the world aboard your sailboat, or just hide away in your cozy mountain cabin.

Passive income allows you to become the master of your own destiny. With money trickling into your bank account automatically every month, you can relax, take a good hard look at your life, and decide exactly what you want to do. For me, that meant spending time with my family, friends, and loved ones. But there's no telling what it might mean for you.

I often think about where my life would be if I hadn't made the switch to passive income and replaced my salary when I did. I'd probably still be battling L.A. traffic every morning to rush to the office, scurrying between "power lunches" and "working dinners" with bigshot celebrities, and struggling to cope with the thousands of daily dramas that come from being a top Hollywood agent. My time and efforts would be in constant demand. I would always have to be ready to put out fires or put my reputation on the line. Taking any time off would only make things worse when I returned. A three-day vacation would set me back three months.

Back then, I was gaining money, but I was losing in other ways. I had less time with my family, less independence, and probably a shorter life expectancy due to all the stress.

I'm glad I said no to the dream job and pursued a life that felt more authentic to me. It took a few years, a lot of research, and a ton of hard work to free myself from the golden handcuffs, but it was the best decision I ever made. I'm thankful for it every day. And I'm so grateful that I now get to spend my time and energy helping other people realize their own independence and take control of their lives too, on their own terms.

Every time one of my clients reaches the point where their passive income surpasses their full-time salary, I personally give them a call to share the news. Hearing the joy, relief, and excitement in their voices never gets old and these calls are one of the best parts of my job. It takes me back to the moment when I first realized I'd successfully replaced my agency salary, and a single thought echoed through my mind: *I'm free*. For you, this moment might come in a few months or a few years. It might take more than a decade. But if you assess and enact the strategies laid forth in this book, it's not a question—you'll get there.

Once you take care of yourself, you can set to work on the rest of your family. I built up more than enough passive income for my future children, and for their children. A person who spends their whole life earning money can certainly amass a fortune. But a person who devotes their days to building passive income will set their family up for many future generations. They will create a fortune that continues to grow on its own for many years after they're gone. I was able to do this and establish long-term security for my family. I've created true generational wealth.

You can do it too, and you don't have to slave away for decades to make it happen. Take my advice and find the passive investment vehicle that works for you. You can start small. Gradually build up your automatic revenue until you've got a machine that can safely sustain you and your family. Commit to developing a passive income strategy, set goals for yourself, make a plan, and just get started. Once you begin to walk this path, you won't want to stop.

They say when you're young you have the potential to do anything, but I think that's just motivational fluff. The reality is, when you're young, you lack the resources and knowledge to master your own life. You need to pay your dues first, struggle, learn, and save up. Only once you've built up capital and experience are you finally ready to take the next step and do 'anything.'

At least, that's how it was for me. I wasn't graced with a massive trust fund or inheritance. My parents didn't build a passive income machine for me to take advantage of. I had to find my own way. Today, my generational income machine operates itself. All I have to do is grease the cogs, replace old parts, and make sure the pistons keep firing. For the first time in my life, the world is truly my oyster.

And yet, I still choose to work. It might seem strange that I've earned enough money to do as I please and I haven't quit my job and moved to the Bahamas just yet. But the truth is, I'm in love with what I've created, and I want to share it with as many people as possible. I believe that anyone can achieve this freedom and I want to give other people the tools to reach total independence for themselves. So please, if these strategies work for you, let me know about it. Send an email to team@fourpeakspartners.com and tell us your story. I love to hear from people who have benefited from my writings.

However, building passive income is not for everybody. Not everyone craves a strong sense of independence. Not everyone is willing to do the work, learn the skills, and save their money. Some people like to stay in line, follow a normal routine, and live a modest life without pushing themselves too hard or thinking too critically.

Does that sound like you?

I can assume that, since you've reached the end of this book, you're ready to rise up and grab life by the reins. You're ready for change. You're thinking about the future and planning how to make it work in your favor.

You're not here to make a few lemons into lemonade...you're ready to plant a whole damn orchard.

There is more content for this book that wasn't ready when the manuscript was sent to print. To read the "Lost Chapter" which contains all of the extra tips and tricks I didn't have time to get to in this book, visit our website at **passiveincomethebook.com** and I'll send you the entire chapter for free. You can also find a series of videos there where I explain exactly how to build a passive income machine step by step and links to listen to my podcast, *The Impatient Investor*.

Made in the USA
Middletown, DE
15 June 2023

32694704R00130